Stop Choosing to Be Broke:

A User's Guide to Money

JAROM J. BERGESON

Copyright © 2023 Jarom J. Bergeson

All rights reserved.

No portion of this book may be reproduced in any form without written permission from the publisher or author, except as permitted by U.S. copyright law.

This publication is designed to provide accurate and authoritative information in regard to the subject matter covered. It is sold with the understanding that neither the author nor the publisher is engaged in rendering legal, investment, accounting or other professional services. While the publisher and author have used their best efforts in preparing this book, they make no representations or warranties with respect to the accuracy or completeness of the contents of this book and specifically disclaim any implied warranties of merchantability or fitness for a particular purpose. No warranty may be created or extended by sales representatives or written sales materials. The advice and strategies contained herein may not be suitable for your situation. You should consult with a professional when appropriate. Neither the publisher nor the author shall be liable for any loss of profit or any other commercial damages, including but not limited to special, incidental, consequential, personal, or other damages.

ISBN: 979-8-218-32033-1

DEDICATION

To everyone who believes they can't take control of their finances and build lasting wealth. You absolutely can – but no one can do it for you!

CONTENTS

	Acknowledgments	i
1	Build Wealth Without Sacrificing Financial Peace	1
2	You Can Wander Into Debt …	6
3	… But You'll Never Wander Out	16
4	Step One – Save a Starter Emergency Fund of (at least) $1,000	32
5	Step Two – Pay Off All Debt Except the House Using the Debt Snowball (or Some Variation Thereof)	36
6	Step Three – Save 3–6 Months of Expenses in a Fully Funded Emergency Fund	65
7	Step Four – Invest (about) 15% of Your Household Income for Retirement	74
8	Step Five – Save for Your Children's College Fund	94
9	Step Six – Pay Off Your Home Early	109
10	Step Seven – Build Wealth and Be Generous!	132

ACKNOWLEDGMENTS

I have to start by thanking Mark Kohler and Mat Sorensen, my incredible bosses at KKOS Lawyers, who allowed me to follow my passion and write a book on this topic. Also, they don't know me, but I need to thank Dave Ramsey and his team at Ramsey Solutions. Before I started following them, I was a financial ship without a rudder. As you will see, there are plenty of times I feel like things can be done differently than how Dave preaches, but his work and ethic permeate this entire book. Finally, a special thanks to my wife and kids, who put up with me day in and day out – I love you guys!

1

BUILD WEALTH WITHOUT SACRIFICING FINANCIAL PEACE

"How much debt do you have?" As a tax attorney who has practiced in the field for over a decade, I ask this question almost every day. It comes up when clients ask whether they should borrow money to purchase an investment property or expand their business. Sometimes, it's because I have a client with stars in their eyes about maxing out their retirement account contributions, starting a business, or buying their first rental property when they are still drowning in credit card, car, and/or student loan debt. I ask it before I discuss the virtues of avoiding debt in the first place or eliminating debt before making any aggressive investment or business moves.

Asking this question makes me and the law firm I work for (KKOS Lawyers) unique. Most tax attorneys are concerned with how debt might affect the structure or taxation associated with the particular deal they are looking at. At KKOS, we are a bit different. We take a holistic approach. We are concerned with the total financial health of our clients. We can help our clients create a tax-efficient investment structure that may have excellent returns. But if we ignore (or are unaware of) the fact that the client has a mountain of consumer debt going into a potential investment, we are not doing the best job we can for them.

Making intelligent investments (in real estate, the stock market, cryptocurrency, etc.) is how we build wealth in this country. However, spending money to invest when you are carrying credit card, auto loan, and/or student loan balances can turn every tenant default, bank failure, or Sam Bankman-Fried into a personal financial crisis (especially if you also borrowed the money to invest). An investment made while mired in debt is not a smart investment. It may work out, but just like winning the lottery, if it happens, it's because you were lucky – not because you were smart.

So, while we never give specific advice about what investments to purchase or sell, we absolutely counsel our clients on when it makes sense to invest, why eliminating consumer debt before investing is the best policy, and how to get out of debt as quickly as possible.

The guiding principle I use when walking clients through their finances (as well as in handling my own) is, "Build wealth – but don't sacrifice financial peace in the process." Ok, that sounds great, but what exactly does it mean? I think it's four main things:

1) **Make <u>intentional</u> financial decisions – and first and foremost, choose to live on less than you make.** Sounds simple, right? But, when 83% of Americans own at least one credit card[1], 56% of active credit card users carry a balance[2], our collective credit card debt is $1.031 Trillion[3], and 57% of us don't have enough cash on hand to cover a $1,000 emergency[4], maybe it isn't so simple – or perhaps we choose to make it more complicated than it needs to be. My wife

---

[1] https://www.zippia.com/advice/credit-card-statistics/
[2] https://www.lendingtree.com/credit-cards/credit-card-debt-statistics/
[3] https://www.lendingtree.com/credit-cards/credit-card-debt-statistics/
[4] https://fortune.com/recommends/banking/57-percent-of-americans-cant-afford-a-1000-emergency-expense/

and I sit down together and create a budget every month. We make conscious, intentional, mutual decisions about our money. We give every dollar an assignment. We make those assignments in order of importance based on our shared values. In fifty-plus months of doing so, we have never gotten to the end of the money only to find there's more month left to go.

2) **Be skeptical of debt.** I advocate for avoiding debt in almost all circumstances. I can confidently state that it <u>never</u> makes sense to use debt to purchase something you will consume (like a meal or a vacation) or that will go down in value (like clothing, a car, or a boat). Using debt to finance the purchase of a home, an investment property, an education, or a business (you know, things that can actually make you money) can make sense – but only within specific parameters that we will explore in this book. I practice what I preach in this regard. I have no car, credit card, or student loan debt. My mortgage is my only monthly payment, and it's less than 10% of our total monthly take-home pay. My wife and I have sworn a joint blood oath (only sort of kidding) NEVER to incur any non-mortgage debt again. My default position (which is part of my DNA now) is to avoid debt.

3) **Don't try to keep up with the Joneses.** It's not worth it, and you'll end up chasing something you'll never find. I love my job, and I make a pretty good living. Yet, I roll into the office each day in a sweet (and paid-for) 2009 Toyota Prius with nearly 160,000 miles. My wife's vehicle is a luxurious (and paid-for) 2011 Toyota Sienna minivan with about 180,000 miles. We will likely both get new cars in the next two to three years – but we will buy used and pay cash. We don't own a boat, a camper trailer, a side-by-side, or any ATVs. We have no toys – and thus, no need for a "toy hauler." If we ever want any of those things, we will save up

and pay cash for them. We have a comfortable home we bought in 2016. We'd like to renovate and add on to get some extra space. We plan to do so in the next three to five years – without incurring any debt (even though we'd be approved for a home equity loan on the spot if we applied). The purpose of our vacations is to take our kids to fun and educational locations – not to impress people we don't really like (or frankly, even know) on social media (we're Gen Xers, so we're too old to care much about that anyway) – so we cash-flow our trips 100%. We buy nice clothes for ourselves and our kids, but we are infinitely more likely to pick up something on clearance at Kohl's than to drop $250 on a hoodie at Lululemon. We eat out a few times each month. However, our restaurant destinations are more likely to have drive-thrus than white linen tablecloths. <u>Comparison is the thief of joy</u>. How do you stop the thief? <u>Stop comparing</u>. Start living with joy and gratitude for what you have and the opportunity each day brings to improve and do more.

4) **Choose peace.** You may be thinking, "Jarom, you don't have a huge house, a fancy car, or a killer speedboat. You don't take exotic vacations. It sounds like you make most of your retail purchases at Walmart. So, what exactly do you have, and why on earth should I listen to you?" Those are great (and completely valid) questions. Here is my response – I have five months of living expenses in the bank, earning interest. I have a growing retirement fund I add to from every paycheck. I have savings in place to help my kids go to college without incurring any student loan debt. At the end of the month, I don't have to decide which bills to pay. Instead, I have to decide how much of the monthly surplus (after already saving for retirement and college) goes into the new car fund and how much goes into the home renovation fund. <u>I have financial peace</u>. I don't wake up in a cold sweat, wondering how I'll be able to pay all my bills if I lose my

job. I don't stress about every dip in the stock or housing market (or every rise in interest rates — in fact, rising rates are actually my friend!). I don't worry about how to pay for a major car repair or an unexpected medical bill. My financial well-being does not hinge on whether some politician decides it is politically expedient to forgive my student loans (or whether a panel of judges determines that politician's decision is unconstitutional). I have taken that part of my life out of the government's hands. When it comes to my finances, the decisions made in my house are infinitely more important than those made in the White House. Does it feel good to be in that position? Why, yes. Yes, it does.

I don't tell you these things to brag (because everybody brags about their 2009 Prius, right?) — I do it to make sure you know that change (radical, life-altering change) is possible. It wasn't always like this for us. <u>As of August 2019, my wife and I had $221,000 in non-mortgage debt</u>. It broke down like this:

- $171,000 in student loan debt (thank you, private graduate school tuition!).
- $47,000 in car debt (on a brand-new 2018 Toyota Sienna we literally drove off the showroom floor and that sweet 2009 Toyota Prius).
- $3,000 in debt on furniture and cell phones.

We didn't exactly live paycheck to paycheck, but there were <u>several</u> months where, despite an income well into six figures, my wife had to tell me (because she kept track of our finances), "Hey, we can't spend any more money until you get paid next week." <u>I always hated it when she said that</u> — but for years, I didn't hate it enough to change anything.

So, how did we get from August 2019 to today? A full explanation requires going back a bit further.

2

YOU CAN WANDER INTO DEBT …

I was born into a fairly typical middle-class family in the late 1970s. I am the oldest of four kids. My dad got his accounting degree, passed the CPA Exam, and went to work for various companies and accounting firms in downtown Denver, Colorado, in the early 1980s. My mom picked up some overnight janitorial work now and again, but she was primarily a stay-at-home mom. I remember getting our first microwave and VCR when most people already had them. Our vacations were usually at grandma's house, and we ate a lot of tuna fish sandwiches and canned soup.

However, as the '80s wore on and became the '90s, we moved from Denver to Phoenix, Arizona, and my dad's career took off. By the mid-'90s, he was the CEO of a managed healthcare company that United Healthcare would eventually purchase. Because it was the '90s, my mom got a brand-new conversion van to haul us around, and my dad drove a brand-new Audi 100 (which I inherited after four years when I got my driver's license). I had my pick of the finest (and most expensive) sneakers Foot Locker had to offer when it came time to buy shoes. We took vacations to Disney World and Hawaii. We ate out a lot. We moved into a 4,500-square-foot home. What I'm getting at is that we were "normal" by American standards. My dad was making a lot of money for the time, but we were doing a good job of spending just about all of it. My parents are amazing people, but they are both spenders at heart, and we never really talked much about finances or debt or how to deal with money.

I graduated from high school in 1996 and earned a scholarship to study Broadcast Journalism at Brigham Young University (BYU). My parents covered all my other expenses that first year. This was my first time away from home, and I injected that freedom into my veins like heroin. I stayed up late, slept in even later, smuggled caffeinated soda onto the campus of the #1 "Stone Cold Sober" school in the United States[5], missed a lot of class, and promptly lost my scholarship.

When I returned to Provo after my two-year mission in Portugal for the Church of Jesus Christ of Latter-day Saints, things were dramatically different financially for my family. The reasons why are unimportant, but my parents were no longer able to pay much of anything toward my tuition. As chronicled above, my scholarship was gone. So, the two ways I financed school before my mission (my scholarship and cash infusions from Mommy and Daddy) were gone.

I would like to tell you that I pulled myself up by the bootstraps, got two jobs, and cash-flowed my way through my undergraduate degree. That would not be accurate. Instead, I filled out a FAFSA, qualified for some small grants, applied for a credit card, and got a (very) part-time job. I also took out my very first student loan. In doing so, I joined the 54% of adults with student loan debt who accepted those loans without estimating what the monthly payment would be when it came time to start paying them back[6].

---

[5] https://news.byu.edu/announcements/22-years-stone-cold-sober
[6] https://www.incharge.org/financial-literacy/data/student-loan-credit-card-debt-statistics-nfcs/

<u>I began "wandering" into debt. I made a decision not to put much thought into my financial decisions</u>. After quite a bit of messing around at the beginning of the new millennium, I (finally) graduated from BYU with a Broadcast Journalism degree in 2004. When I did, I had accumulated about $10,000 in student loan debt and $3,000 in credit card debt. I was not an outlier. Today, about 55% of folks with four-year degrees graduate with student debt, and the average debt load is over $28,000[7]. As of 2021, 65% of college students have some form of credit card debt, with an average balance of $3,280[8].

Shortly before graduating from BYU, I decided I wanted to attend law school. I did so primarily because although the sports talk radio station I interned for in Salt Lake City offered to hire me as a producer, they could only guarantee me thirty hours per week and could only offer me $7.50/hour. Because that wasn't much better than working in fast food, I moved back home to Phoenix, started studying for the LSAT, and got a job answering customer service calls for a well-known stock brokerage firm. Living at home and having a full-time job allowed me to pay off my credit card debt and make a little headway on my student loans before beginning law school at the University of Denver in 2005.

Starting law school, on the other hand, allowed me to pause any payments on my undergraduate student debt. It also gave me the opportunity to take out more student loans – <u>a lot more student loans</u>. Because I didn't think there was any other way (and because the process was shockingly easy), I chose to take out those loans. As a result, even though I got a paying job with the federal government during my third year of law school, I racked up over $130,000 in additional student loan debt. Why? Because it was the path of least resistance (at least at the time). I am not alone. As of

---

[7] https://www.nerdwallet.com/article/loans/student-loans/student-loan-debt
[8] https://collegefinance.com/research/college-student-debt-and-credit-card-usage

2020, 95% of law students took out at least some student loans to graduate, and their average debt was about $165,000[9].

And that wasn't all! During law school, I also took on $16,500 in credit card debt to finance my lifestyle. Throughout this period, I chose not to worry about how much I was spending (or what I was spending it on) – even though my income varied from absolutely nothing to very little. If I wanted to go out to eat (and going out to eat is my jam), I did – and I put it on credit. If I wanted to go home to Utah over Thanksgiving, I did – and I put it on credit. If I wanted to purchase Denver Broncos season tickets (which I fell into an opportunity to do in 2006), I did – and I put it on credit. I chose not to think about the consequences. My thought process was not, "Hey, I will be an attorney soon – I'll pay off all this debt in no time!" It was more, "This is just how people live – I'm doing what everybody else does." Whether, when, and how I would repay the debt didn't even cross my mind.

Toward the end of my second year of law school, I started dating an adorable girl from Smithfield, Utah. She was about to get her Master's in Social Work from the University of Denver. We got married about a year later – two months before I graduated from law school. She comes from a much more conservative financial background than I do – but she still had about $70,000 in student loan debt from graduate school when we got married. That was her only debt. She hated my credit card debt, and even though we didn't make much at the time, we were able to knock out that $16,500 in debt in about 12 months. We have never carried a credit card balance since.

My in-laws had been 100% debt-free (including their home) for about ten years by the time I married their daughter, and my wife was able to avoid debt until she went to graduate school. However,

---

[9]https://www.americanbar.org/content/dam/aba/administrative/young_law yers/2020-student-loan-survey.pdf

she married a pretty persuasive guy, so I convinced her that it didn't matter what we did — we would be in student loan debt for the (very) long haul. Therefore, we should do whatever we could to pay as little as humanly possible on those loans. This would allow us maximum financial flexibility going forward. She agreed, and we were on our way (to nowhere — as it turned out).

We spent the next few years being "normal." We certainly weren't extravagant — my wife wouldn't stand for that. However, we financed our cars (I mean, who actually has $25k in cash?), and we bought furniture and phones on credit (after all, there's no interest!). It's the American Way — if you can "afford the payment," you can have it — right now. No need to wait or save up — instant gratification!

During that time, I got the job I have now — at KKOS Lawyers in Cedar City, Utah. As I grew and learned and the firm became more successful, I started to earn more. In fact, from 2011 to 2019, my income nearly tripled, but somehow, our overall financial picture remained about the same. <u>As a wise man once said, "You can't outearn stupid.</u>" We just kept making financial decisions without a compass or much of a defined purpose. We spent almost everything we made and didn't have much to show for it.

We never did a monthly budget — and this was my fault. My wife would have done one every month — but I refused. <u>I thought budgets were for two types of people: geeks and morons</u>. In my head, you only did a budget if you were either a pencil-pushing nerd or someone too dumb to know where you stood as you went. "We're not overdrawn. We don't carry a credit card balance. Why would we need a budget?" It never occurred to me that the reason we periodically ran out of money at the end of the month might have something to do with my refusal to budget. It's not rocket science — but "denial" isn't just a river in Egypt.

As a result, we just sort of treaded water. Every time our income increased, we would do something dumb – like borrowing over $40,000 to purchase a brand-new minivan in November 2018. The $650 payment on that van brought our combined minimum monthly debt payment (on student, auto, furniture, and cell phone loans) to just under $2,800 – almost twice the amount of our monthly mortgage payment. This was despite KKOS Lawyers purchasing Dave Ramsey's *Financial Peace University* for all employees in 2016. I went through the class – but only half-heartedly. I didn't hate it. But I felt like it didn't apply to me because there was nothing I could do about my student loan debt (it was just too big), and I didn't have any of the "genuinely evil" high-interest credit card debt – which (in my mind anyway) was the real problem.

So, there we were – early 2019. The van we bought on credit pushed our household debt (not including the house) to about $220,000. Our cars might have fetched $40,000 if we tried to sell them. Depending on what point in the month you looked, we would have had somewhere between $1,000 and $10,000 in the bank. The stuff in our house might have sold for another $15,000. I had made some 401k contributions, and my wife had an old 401k she had rolled to an IRA, so we had about $45,000 in retirement savings. We had about $60,000 of equity in our home. <u>Add it all up, carry the one, and our household net worth (when I was 41 and my wife was 43) was NEGATIVE $55,000 – all on an annual income closer to $200,000 than $100,000</u>.

Who was to blame for this state of affairs? With apologies to Ms. T. Swift, "<u>It's me. Hi. I'm the problem. It's me.</u>" There was no one to blame but myself. It wasn't the fault of the various Democratic and Republican administrations that had occupied the White House during my adult life. It wasn't Wells Fargo's or Capital One's fault. It wasn't the fault of the University of Denver or Brigham Young University. It wasn't my parent's fault – and it certainly wasn't my wife's fault. I made the decisions that got us into the mess. It was on me. <u>If your current situation looks like mine did in early 2019, then stare directly in the mirror and say it with me, "It's me. Hi. I'm the problem. It's me."</u>

<u>You are the problem (and so was I). That's the bad news. The good news? You are also the solution!</u> Just like they didn't cause the problem, the occupant of the White House, the banks, the universities, your mom, your spouse – none of these people will fix it. Cleaning up the mess is going to be on you. I can promise you that you are up to the task (even if you don't think you are)! You are stronger (and smarter) than you give yourself credit for! Don't give up just because the task looks overwhelming. If you are motivated and have a plan, you can tackle whatever you are facing!

Another interesting fact is that <u>I had no idea exactly how much debt we had at that point</u>. Avoiding that information was my coping mechanism. I didn't want to know. I knew the number was bad, but I didn't want to know how bad. I thought I knew two things about that number: 1) It was so large it would be overwhelming even to think about, and 2) There was nothing I could do to make it go away quicker. Given those two "facts," what would be the point of knowing the exact amount of our debt? It would only make me depressed. <u>I also didn't know how long it would take to pay everything off</u>. I had a general idea, but I didn't know for sure. Again, given my attitude about the debt, what good would that information be? One day – decades in the future – it would be gone. That was good enough for me.

Fast forward to the Summer of 2019. The YouTube algorithm started suggesting Dave Ramsey and *Ramsey Show* videos to me for some reason. I ended up watching a few each day. As I did, I found Mr. Ramsey engaging and entertaining, so I kept watching. Besides, I liked to ridicule the "idiots" who called in for advice about what to do with their credit card debt. Being free of credit card debt, I felt like I had my life together a bit more than those folks. I also watched a few "Debt Free Scream" videos. These are the segments of the *Ramsey Show* where people who have paid off tens or hundreds of thousands in debt in relatively short timeframes travel to Ramsey Solutions' studio in Tennessee to tell their stories live on the air. At the end of the segment, Dave allows them to scream that they are "debt freeeeeee!!!" Back then, the Debt Free Scream videos were not my favorite. In many cases, I frankly felt like the people were lying. <u>I thought, "There is no way these people paid off that much debt that fast while making that much." Turns out I was wrong</u>.

Each year in early August, my wife takes the kids to her parents' home in Smithfield, Utah, so they can attend the Cache County Fair and Rodeo. Because I grew up in Denver and Phoenix (i.e., large cities), the Fair and Rodeo is not really my thing. I usually take advantage of my wife and kids' absence to stay late at the office and catch up on work. However, on August 7, 2019, I started binging *Ramsey Show* videos instead. It turned out to be a life-changing decision. You can call it whatever you'd like, but I believe it was God intervening in my life. <u>As I watched, two thoughts hit me and would not go away: 1) "Dude, these people aren't idiots – you are the idiot! You're making well into six figures, and your wife has to tell you to be careful about your spending at the end of the month!" and 2) "You make too much money to be this damn broke!"</u>

Many of us need to take steps to increase our income. These steps may include obtaining additional education or training, being aware of other opportunities outside the walls of our current workplaces, or taking on a side hustle or second job. However, if you are reading this, there's an excellent chance that your income is already pretty good – but you have made some silly (or at least unintentional) financial decisions and wandered into financial peril. <u>More and more money comes in, but you don't have much to show for it. You feel like you aren't making any headway. At worst, you are drowning, and at best, you are just treading water. If this describes you, then let me say it for you – you make too much</u>

money to be this damn broke! The good news is that there is a way out! I have traveled it, and so can you!

That afternoon, for the first time since graduating from law school (over 11 years earlier), I took a look at my student loan balances and how many months we had left to pay. I had a rough idea of the balances, but seeing them in black and white was startling. I did the math and figured out that if we only made minimum student loan payments, we would make the last payment when I was 55, and my wife was 57 (again, we were 41 and 43 at the time). That was my breaking point. It was the moment when I became "sick and tired of being sick and tired." I simply could not stomach that idea. Where it was previously just a fact of life, it suddenly became unacceptable. There was no way in hell I was going to remain in student loan debt for another 14 years. I felt like a charge of electricity had been sent through my body. I was on fire. I immediately sent my wife the following text:

> Don't know why, but I'm amped up on Dave Ramsey right now. We need to do a budget and stick to it. We make enough that we shouldn't just be treading water. I don't want to pay student loans until I'm 55. We need to start knocking out smallest debts first and rolling it into the next. No more putting anything on payments (even if there's no interest). Limit eating out and other crap. People are going to think we're crazy, but if we do it I think we can be out of debt (other than the house) in 3-4 years.

When I sent that text, my wife was at Old Navy buying school clothes for our kids. She called me right back, and we talked about what was happening. Luckily, we were generally on the same page. There were details to iron out – and believe me, some of them would take some serious ironing, but our lives would never be the same. That's why August 7, 2019 is known as D (Dave Ramsey)

Day at our house. We celebrate it every year by eating rice and beans – Dave's "favorite" meal (because it's cheap)!

3

... BUT YOU'LL NEVER WANDER OUT

No one gets much of anywhere without a plan. A football team can have superior athletes at every position, but without a competent game plan to attack the opposition on both sides of the ball (offense and defense), all that talent is wasted. It's no different when it comes to getting out of debt (or your financial well-being in general). A healthy income is great (and is totally helpful) – but without a competent game plan on both sides of the ball (maximizing income (offense) and minimizing expenses (defense)), all that money coming in will be wasted. Need proof? <u>A 2009 *Sports Illustrated* article reported that (despite six, seven, and sometimes eight-figure annual incomes), 78% of former NFL players have gone bankrupt or are under financial stress by the time they have been retired for two years</u>[10]. <u>Why? Mainly because they never had a game plan for their money</u>.

Probably the best-known and most widely-used plan for financial freedom and peace is Dave Ramsey's "Baby Steps." There are other plans out there, but:

1) *The Total Money Makeover* (the book where Dave explains the Baby Steps) has sold over five million copies[11];

---

[10] https://vault.si.com/vault/2009/03/23/how-and-why-athletes-go-broke
[11] https://www.ramseysolutions.com/store/bundles/the-total-money-makeover-hardcover-book-workbook

2) Mr. Ramsey's radio show (*The Ramsey Show*) has more than 23 million weekly listeners; and

3) My wife and I used the Baby Steps to eliminate $221,000 in debt in 31 months.

Therefore, we will use Mr. Ramsey's Baby Steps as the framework for obtaining financial health – besides, they just work! So (in all their glory), here are the Baby Steps[12]:

Step One: **Save a Starter Emergency Fund of $1,000.**

Step Two: **Pay Off All Debt (Except the House) Using the Debt Snowball.**

Step Three: **Save 3–6 Months of Expenses in a Fully Funded Emergency Fund.**

Step Four: **Invest 15% of Your Household Income in Retirement.**

Step Five: **Save for Your Children's College Fund.**

Step Six: **Pay Off Your Home Early.**

Step Seven: **Build Wealth and Give.**

These steps are crucial. They are the pillars of your financial game plan, and we will dive into each in more detail. We will also pick up where the Ramsey folks leave off and discuss where some reasonable personalization of how to walk the steps can make sense. However, I don't immediately jump into the Baby Steps when people ask me about getting started. Instead, I ask them, "Do you know the first thing you have to pay if you want to get out of debt?" When they shrug their shoulders or say "no," I tell them,

---

[12] https://www.ramseysolutions.com/dave-ramsey-7-baby-steps

"freaking attention!"

The word that embodies "paying freaking attention" is "intentionality." Being intentional means that you start doing things <u>on purpose</u>. I spent my entire adult life (over twenty years) not paying any freaking attention to my finances. Because I (like, literally never) made intentional, purpose-driven decisions in that area, I fell into trap after trap (credit cards, student loans, car loans, etc.). Consequently, I managed to "wander," quite UNintentionally (and despite several consecutive years of six-figure incomes), into $221,000 of debt and a negative net worth at age 41.

How exactly do you go about becoming intentional when it comes to your finances? Well, in my experience, there are two categories of things we all tend to be intentional about doing:

1) **Things we love.** I <u>love</u> to play golf. I am intermittently pretty good and thoroughly mediocre at it – but I love it. I proactively make plans (and time) to do it. Once I have a tee time, I **<u>never</u>** forget about it. I never just space it and fail to show up. I am always on time. Whether hunting, working on cars, binging shows on Netflix, spending time with family, or whatever – we are all intentional about doing the things we love.

2) **Things that are important to us.** I <u>don't love</u> to work out. I played a ton of basketball through my early 20s, but that was my only source of voluntary exercise. Even though I stopped playing much basketball as a young man, I didn't stop making poor eating choices. Consequently, I put on a fair amount of weight and took great pains to avoid stepping on a scale. At age 28, I finally hopped on one for the first time in about seven years and found that I was one Double Whopper shy of 300 lbs. That experience prompted me to make some significant changes in my life – including working out regularly. I feel better, and my annual checkups

with my doctor are much less stressful when I make it a point to work out. Working out has become <u>important</u> to me. Because it is something I value, I make time for it. I wake up at 5 a.m. each day to make sure I get it done. Even though I don't love it, I make room for it in my life because it is important. I don't miss many days, and I don't make excuses when I do. That way, a missed day doesn't become a missed week, which doesn't become a missed month, which doesn't become quitting entirely. <u>Whether working out, giving our best at work, attending religious services, spending time with our family, or whatever, we are all intentional about doing what we believe is important.</u>

When I finally decided I made too much money to be so damn broke and refused to spend the next 14 years paying student loans, making intelligent financial decisions entered category two above (things that are important) for the first time in my life. So, I started making financial decisions <u>on purpose</u>. I broke through the imaginary barriers in my head and looked at our total debt for the first time in years. I sat down with my wife, and we listed our debts so we could wrap our heads around them. Most importantly, I attempted a monthly budget for the first time ever. If you are reading this book, it is likely because making intelligent financial decisions has also become important to you (or maybe someone in your life thinks it should be), and you are ready to be intentional in your finances.

<u>Nothing will force you to be intentional about your money choices like a budget</u>. People always talk about "making your money work for you." Well, your money can only go to work if you give it a job. It doesn't know what to do on its own. A monthly budget is how you give every dollar you earn a job.

Before we dive into the nuts and bolts of how to do a budget, let's address the elephant in the room. <u>No one likes the word "budget." I know that</u>. It's an inherently unattractive word with an overwhelmingly negative connotation, much like "diet." People associate it with the "three Cs" (cut back, cut out, and can't) as well as the "three Ds" (denial, deprivation, and don't)[13]. I admitted earlier that I always felt budgets were only for idiots and geeks. Therefore, I am totally on board with you calling it something else – something that sounds more sophisticated and less guttural. Call it your "monthly financial plan" or that month's "map to financial freedom." I am in favor of any name that helps you actually get it done. Get as creative as you like! That said, I also want us all to get comfortable with the concept of budgeting. Because of that (and because we're all adults), I will use the terms budget and budgeting. You can handle it – I promise.

I understand that the idea of doing an actual budget may seem overwhelming. If it does, I have some advice from my good friend Phil Knight and his struggling little startup, Nike – just do it! Dive in and get messy (because it will be)! However, it will also absolutely, 100%, without question, be worth it!

I understand that you may still be hesitant. If so, I have a proposal. <u>Just track your spending for one month</u>. Don't change anything else – just pay some freaking attention to where, when, and how you spend your money. Let tracking your spending become the gateway drug to budgeting!

Then, take it one step further. When you review your purchases at the end of the month (which is part of "tracking" your spending), think about <u>why</u> you made each purchase. Was that purchase a need or a want? For every purchase you categorize as a need, I want you to ask a follow-up question – <u>are you sure?</u> When you analyze it, I am confident you'll find that more purchases are wants than you initially thought. For any purchase that is a want, you need to have an honest conversation with yourself about whether (from the perspective of getting to where you really want

---

[13]https://njaes.rutgers.edu/sshw/message/message.php?p=Finance&m=351

to be financially) you would make that purchase again.

Doing a budget will force you to make money decisions based on your priorities. You decide what gets paid first, and those things go at the top of your budget – in order of importance. Let me give you an example – the first line on our budget is (and always has been) tithing. We donate 10% of our income to our church. We are not unique in that. Tithing is a biblical principle that is emphasized in many religious denominations. Tithing is the most important thing for us. We believe that only 90% of what we make really belongs to us. The first 10% belongs to God, and since He is the source of everything we have anyway, giving only 10% back to Him is actually a pretty sweet deal! <u>I'm not saying you need to have the same financial priorities I do, but you do need to figure out what your priorities are. Your monthly budget will be a reflection of those priorities</u>.

Let's talk about how a solid budget works. Here is what to do:

1) **Create a "zero-based budget."** In a zero-based budget, you will use every cent of your income every month. You will allocate all your income across your fixed expenses, needs, wants, giving, saving, and debt. <u>When you are not paying any freaking attention, your money will act like an unsupervised child. At best, it will sit around and not accomplish much. At worst, it will get into a lot of trouble</u>. When you are intentional about your money, you make it behave. You tell it what to do. You accomplish this through your monthly budget.

   Think of your budget as a "chore chart." The chore chart is usually attached to the fridge in households with children. Each child is assigned a list of duties for the day/week/month. Your budget is the monthly chore chart for your money.

2) **Start with your income.** Plug in how much you plan to deposit into your checking account over the next month. If your income is steady, this will be pretty easy. It will be more difficult if your income is seasonal or commission/bonus-based. In that case, you will be doing some estimating. Our income is at least always somewhat variable. I make a base salary and a monthly bonus based on the revenue I generate for the firm, so we have to estimate our total income each month. <u>Pro tip: If your income is variable, be conservative in the estimate you use for your budget</u>. It's always better to set your estimate low and then decide what to do with the surplus at the end of the month than to set it high, spend accordingly, and run out of money before you run out of month.

3) **List your expenses in order of priority.** Taking a tithe or other spiritual obligation out of the equation (because it will not apply to everyone), you should always start with what Mr. Ramsey calls your "Four Walls[14]." The Four Walls are:

   - Food
   - Shelter
   - Utilities
   - Transportation

   Making sure you and your family have food in your bellies, a place to live that has heat, lights, and water, and that you have a way to get to work is paramount. Everything else falls in line behind these four necessities.

   However, what comes next (and in what amounts) will depend on your priorities. <u>You will need to make intentional, value-based decisions on how to spend your money</u>. Is that daily trip to Starbucks more critical than making extra

---

[14] https://www.ramseysolutions.com/budgeting/4-things-you-must-budget

progress on your debt? Are you willing to cut down on DoorDash and eating out so you can put a few hundred extra bucks in your retirement account each month? Is it worth eliminating some streaming subscriptions to allow you to help your kids make it through college without incurring any student loan debt? These are the types of questions your budget will force you to answer.

The budgeting process will require you to review your spending for prior months to estimate what you will spend in each category. If you're anything like us, the experience will be simultaneously enlightening and frightening. I promise you will find places to trim the fat. We did. Here is what we found:

- Our monthly restaurant outlay was several hundred dollars more than we thought. We rectified that immediately.
- I never paid any freaking attention to the fact that we were shelling out almost $200/month for satellite TV. We canceled that as soon as possible and replaced it with a streaming service for less than $70/month.
- We found a great deal on high-speed internet and saved almost $50/month.
- We started paying attention to the grocery store ads and coupons. Armed with that information, we made our grocery-shopping decisions accordingly, saving hundreds of dollars each month.

After a couple of months of preparing and living on a budget, my wife and I looked at each other and said, "Where is all this money coming from?!" Our income hadn't changed, but because we were making intentional decisions to limit our expenses, it felt like we got a raise! When you start this process and dial in your budget, it will feel like you got one, too!

4) **Track your spending.** Okay, you've got that budget/chore chart on the fridge, and you're ready to go. Awesome! However, any parent will tell you a well-thought-out chore chart is only the beginning. The assigned chores will never get done without some serious oversight from mom and dad. It's no different with your budget – and that "parental supervision" comes from you – in tracking your spending. <u>If you only check in on your budget at the beginning and the end of the month, you will fail. I guarantee it</u>. You must track your spending. I suggest doing it before you leave the store parking lot or log out of Amazon, but you should do it at least daily. Otherwise, it will get away from you and become overwhelming. And when something becomes overwhelming, we tend to avoid doing it and eventually give up.

Luckily, this is the 21st Century! You won't need to take a pen and paper on every trip to the store. Technology has provided several apps that take care of the math for you. Because we follow the Ramsey Baby Steps, we use the Ramsey app, EveryDollar. During our debt-free journey, we used the free version, but now we pay for the premium version, which syncs to our bank account and makes tracking our spending extraordinarily simple and easy. EveryDollar also comes preloaded with suggestions for spending categories and keeps track of what you spend in those areas over time.

That said, EveryDollar is certainly not the only game in town. Several apps will help you keep up with your monthly spending. Here are a few:

- Mint
- YNAB

- Goodbudget
- Personal Capital
- PocketGuard
- Fudget

I suggest you take a look at several options. There are also great resources on the web that compare and rate the apps[15]. Don't be scared! Get out there and figure out what works best for you!

5) **Know you will suck at this at first.** I have more confidence in this statement than just about any other in this entire book. You will look back on your first budget and laugh. I know we do! Your estimate of your monthly spending on food, gas, and other necessities will almost certainly be way off. You will forget about all kinds of things you spend money on every month. You will forget that your gas bill increases in the winter and your electric bill increases in the summer. You will forget about things that are only billed once a quarter or once a year. Here's a little secret – that's okay! Don't worry about it – you will get better! I have just as much confidence in this as I do that you will suck at first! Here are a few tips for building a better budget:

- **Figure out the monthly cost of expenses billed quarterly, semi-annually, or annually, and build those monthly costs into your budget.** For us, this includes auto insurance, life insurance, trash service, computer anti-virus protection, etc. This will keep these things from demolishing your budget when they come due. The money will be there when you need it. Revisit these numbers every year to make sure they haven't changed.

---

[15] https://www.nerdwallet.com/article/finance/best-budget-apps; https://www.cnbc.com/select/best-budgeting-apps/

- **Understand that your utility bills will fluctuate from month to month throughout the year depending on how hot or cold it is and how much it rains when you're trying to keep your grass green.** Add up your previous 12 months of gas, electric, and water bills. Divide that number by 12 and put it into your monthly budget. Electricity rates are going up by 8%? Great (ok, not great) – increase that category in your monthly budget by 8%. At the very least, revisit these numbers each year to ensure your monthly allotment to each category still makes sense.

- **Realize that Christmas will happen on December 25 every year – no matter what!** Understand that your loved ones will expect gifts (and those gifts will cost money). Working the estimated cost of Christmas into your monthly budget will allow you to effectively play Santa Claus every December – even if your Christmas Bonus turns out to be a membership in the Jelly of the Month Club (as Cousin Eddie said, "Clark, that's the gift that keeps on giving the whole year!").

- **Estimate the annual cost for seasonal expenses and build those costs into your monthly budget.** If you own a home (and have a yard), you will likely need to budget for things like trees and plants, as well as the maintenance and repair of sprinklers, lawnmowers, weed eaters, etc. Birthdays, anniversaries, and other non-Christmas holidays (I'm looking at you, Valentine's Day) can also sneak up on you if you don't plan for them. So – plan for them!

- **Budget a small amount for "miscellaneous" stuff that doesn't neatly fit into any other category.** You'll be surprised how uncategorized expenses will jump up to bite you. Setting aside a small amount for those things (or to cover cost overruns in other categories) will provide some additional peace.

6) **Breathe in the freedom and enjoy the process.** Living on a budget will bring you freedom (cue the record scratch)! <u>Let me say that again – living on a budget will bring you freedom!</u> "Jarom, you've said some wild stuff in this book, but this takes the cake! How will a set of rules about how much money I can and can't spend each month (and what I can spend it on) bring me freedom? That's crazy talk!" Is it? Consider this:

- **I never have to wonder whether I can afford something.** Either the contemplated purchase fits within the budget (that I made with my wife, based on our shared values), or it doesn't. If it fits and I want it, hit my debit card, baby! If it doesn't, I'm moving on. <u>I call this freedom from buyer's remorse</u>. I might regret buying something because it ended up being poor quality and it wasn't worth what I paid, but I never regret buying something because I overextended myself. Because I make and live on a budget, genuine buyer's remorse isn't something I have to worry about.

- **I don't fear the end of the month – I look forward to it.** Why? Because that's when my budget gives me <u>the freedom to spend</u>. It's the 30th, and there's $75 left in the restaurant budget? Sweet! Let's go out! It's the 29th, and there's $50 left for clothing? Let's go to Old Navy (or wherever it's cool to shop these days)! I can even move money from one category to another. Maybe the entertainment budget is shot, but there's money left for gas at the end of the month. Move it over, and let's go to the movies!

> Here's the secret sauce – as you make and live on a budget and see the progress you are making – creating a monthly budget will move from something you do because you know it is important to something you do because you love doing it. That's how it is for my wife and me. We love doing our budget each month because we love the freedom it provides. We feel financially naked without it! We love tracking our progress toward our shared financial goals. We love the ability it gives us to connect and make our marriage stronger. I don't know if it makes me a geek or a moron (or both), but I love to budget!

I'd also like to say something about accountability. Becoming intentional about your finances will bear more fruit if you regularly report to someone (honestly) about your progress. It's much easier to lie to yourself than to lie to someone else. Find a friend, sibling, or parent to fill that role if you're single. You can join Dave Ramsey's Financial Peace University, and they will provide you with an accountability partner. Many religious and community organizations have programs that can help (the Church of Jesus Christ of Latter-day Saints' Self-Reliance Courses are fantastic in this regard).

However, if you are married, your spouse is your built-in accountability partner. And here's another guarantee – this process will only work if you and your spouse join forces and do it together. I cannot emphasize this enough – one spouse cannot (and should not) pull all the weight in this journey. My wife would have walked down this path years earlier, but I was not on board, so it never happened. However, once we got on the same page, we were unstoppable!

This isn't to say we were (or are) in lock-step on all our financial decisions. One line item on that very first budget gave me a knot in my stomach. It was the $650 loan payment on the van we had purchased just nine months earlier (and the $40,000 in debt it represented). The new me hated that we bought that van and had that payment. I wanted it gone as soon as possible. The problem was that my wife loved that van. She loved how comfortable it was for us and the kids. She loved the new car smell. It was the perfect vehicle for our family.

I sent my wife a text only ten days into our debt-free journey. In that text, I said that if we were serious about getting out of debt, we needed to sell the van and replace it with something (much, much) less expensive. I told her I knew it sucked, and I knew she hated the thought of it. I also told her I knew she knew it was the right thing to do. It would knock almost $25,000 off our debt (we would need to borrow to purchase the replacement van and to pay off the difference between the sale price of our current van and what we owed on it), and it would free up about $450 per month to throw at our debt. I concluded the text by providing her with a link to an online listing for what seemed like a completely reasonable replacement van for under $7,000. I felt I had made a pretty compelling argument.

My wife's three-word response appeared on my phone within ten seconds – "Umm … hell no." I knew I was in trouble. <u>My wife never uses that word</u>. I called her immediately. We discussed both the emotions and the math involved. She was still not on board. I reiterated that I knew she knew this was the right thing to do, but I would wait until she was ready.

It turns out her biggest hangup was the ultra-cheap replacement I suggested. Within a few days, she started sending me links to replacement vans that would be acceptable to her. Within three weeks of that initial text, we had sold our white 2018 AWD Toyota Sienna with 10,000 miles. We replaced it with a white 2011 AWD Toyota Sienna with 100,000 miles. For a few days, we had both vehicles in our driveway before the sale of the 2018 van closed. Our neighbor's six-year-old asked us if our van had a baby!

Marriage is about compromise. Did my wife still have misgivings about selling the 2018 van? Yes. Did she cry when the new owner drove it away? You bet. Would I rather have purchased a replacement for $7-$8,000 instead of the $14,000 we spent? Absolutely. But that's where we landed. I was content to knock $17,000 off our total debt and free up about $400/month toward our remaining debts. My wife was content to drive a more reliable (and considerably less ratty) replacement van than the ones I wanted to look at. Our kids were thrilled because the replacement 2011 van had a DVD player (our 2018 van didn't). Isn't it funny how the kids always come out on top?

With the Baby Steps as the playbook and our monthly budget as the game plan, we began our intentional journey out of debt in August 2019. <u>Through hard work, sacrifice, making adjustments, and ultimately just saying "no" to many things we would have otherwise done or purchased, we made our final debt payment in March 2022. We slayed $221,000 in debt in 31 months! I hit "submit" on that last student loan payment at age 43 (instead of age 55)</u>.

Being intentional (paying freaking attention and acting accordingly) is the key. Mr. Ramsey often uses this anecdote. When they interview the winning quarterback at the end of the Super Bowl and ask him how he and his team did it, the answer is never, "I don't know, it just sort of happened. I wasn't really paying much attention!" Of course it isn't! That would be absurd! The answer is always something to the effect of, "We have been working for this our entire lives! Our guys have been laser-focused and dedicated since training camp, and no one can say they outworked us!" Winning the Super Bowl takes tremendous intentional hard work, sacrifice, and dedication. So does winning with money and really with anything in life. When your interactions with your family, your friends, your co-workers, your neighbors, and yes, your money are all purposeful and thoughtful – the world is an entirely different place.

(In almost all cases) you have the choice to stop being broke, so:

Stop Choosing

- **To bury your head in the sand about your finances.** Believe it or not, ignoring the situation won't make it better.

- **To spend without thinking.** Like eating (or texting), spending solely on emotion will not yield productive results.

- **Hate and fear when it comes to the concept of budgeting.** Budgeting = control. Go ahead, be a control freak!

Start Choosing

- **To pay freaking attention to what's happening with your money.** This is your first and most critical debt payment.

- **Intentional decisions about your money.** Your finances (and your life) will look more like you'd hoped when you start "happening" to things instead of letting them happen to you.

- **Freedom.** To paraphrase a much higher source: "If you continue in making a budget and tracking your spending, then you are my (financial) disciples indeed. And you shall know the truth (about your finances) – and the truth shall make you free[16]!"

---

[16] John 8:31-32

4

STEP ONE - SAVE A STARTER EMERGENCY FUND OF (AT LEAST) $1,000

Okay, so you've experienced your "I've had it" moment. You are sick and tired of barely keeping your head above water. You are ready to make intentional and purpose-driven financial decisions, kick your debt to the curb, and start living! Where do you begin?! <u>Step One is to save (at least) $1,000 in a "Starter" emergency fund</u>.

I want you to have a buffer between you and the silly little things that life can throw at you. If you need a couple of new tires or to get on a plane and go somewhere last minute, I don't want you to be required to borrow money to do it. <u>Your credit card is a crappy emergency fund</u>. Over the long term, you want an emergency fund that will cover major car repairs, medical bills, a job loss, etc. You will tackle that larger fund in Step Three. Your Step One emergency fund is there to cover the little things temporarily while you get out of debt.

For many, this is a step we can immediately check off because we already have that much saved. However, that certainly isn't true across the board. 57% of Americans don't have enough saved to cover a $1,000 emergency[17]. If you find yourself in that 57%, there

---

[17] https://fortune.com/recommends/banking/57-percent-of-americans-cant-afford-a-1000-emergency-expense/

are two ways to knock this out. You can:

- Cut your expenses; or
- Increase your income.

Either one will work – and you may want or need to do both. Unless you are in genuinely dire financial straits, this shouldn't take long (maybe 1-2 months). Only eat rice and beans and ramen for a few weeks, deliver pizzas, turn down the thermostat, drive Uber, live with only one streaming subscription for a while, sell some vintage clothes, donate plasma – there are all kinds of things you can do (and not do) to get that $1,000 saved in a hurry.

On the other side of the coin, a (very) common hangup for people on Step One is being willing to trim back their emergency fund to $1,000. If you already have more than $1,000 saved but also have non-mortgage debt, the Ramsey plan would be to take everything over $1,000 and throw it at that debt. For many (okay, most) people, a $1,000 emergency fund does not seem like enough. "I want more than $1,000 standing between my family and the wolves at the door!" If that's your gut reaction, guess what – your instincts are right! $1,000 isn't enough! I know that a $1,000 emergency fund exposes you to the financial elements – but there is a method to the madness. I want you to feel the urgency of such a slim emergency fund. The thinking is that you are more likely to be serious (and seriously intense) about getting out of debt if you don't have a comfortable emergency fund.

However, the $1,000 emergency fund creates an interesting paradox. What happens when someone with a $1,000 emergency fund has a $2,000 emergency? Chances are they will borrow the remaining $1,000 (on a credit card, from mom and dad, or (heaven forbid) from a payday lender). Being forced to borrow more money when you are laser-focused on eliminating debt can be discouraging (to say the least). It may even cause you to give up. So, having a larger emergency fund can help keep you out of debt.

Also, remember that Mr. Ramsey introduced his Baby Steps in the early 1990s. In the ensuing 30 years, inflation has steadily eroded the purchasing power of the original $1,000 emergency fund he recommended. In fact, $1,000 in 1992 would equal more than $2,100 today[18].

Given this reality, <u>even if you want to "go lean" on your starter emergency fund, I think it should be at least $2,000 – especially if you have kids</u>. There are infinitely more potential emergencies so long as little Noah won't stop climbing trees and so long as kids continue to bring home every illness anyone else in their class has happened to contract.

A second school of thought (advocated in the Self-Reliance Courses taught by the Church of Jesus Christ of Latter-day Saints and others) does not set a particular dollar amount for the starter emergency fund. Instead, these resources recommend saving an initial emergency fund equal to one month of expenses. This is what we did. We felt like it was a good balance. It gave us enough wiggle room that a fairly severe emergency wouldn't require us to use a credit card – but it was small enough that it helped motivate us to plow through our debt as quickly as possible. We went with the larger emergency fund because we knew it would take us multiple years to get out of debt, and having such a flimsy emergency fund for such a long period scared us to death. So, if you anticipate being out of debt in less than a year, the smaller $2,000 emergency fund could make sense.

One twist is that at the end of our debt-free journey, we went ahead and drained our emergency fund to $1,000. We used the extra money to finish paying off our debt. This allowed us to complete the process about two months quicker than would have otherwise been possible. Approaching it this way eliminated our fear of the "long-term" $1,000 emergency fund. We knew we

---

[18] https://www.inflationtool.com/us-dollar/1992-to-present-value

wouldn't stay at $1,000 for long (because being debt-free allowed us to throw relatively large monthly sums onto our "big kid" emergency fund (Step Three) immediately).

Stop Choosing

- **To live life without a financial safety net.** There should be some amount of money in your bank account (at least $1,000) that is "behind the glass" – and you only break the glass in the case of a legitimate emergency.

- **To break the glass for something dumb.** A little financial discipline will go a long way. A Taco Bell craving that can only be satisfied through DoorDash is not an emergency.

- **To use a credit card or a line of credit as your emergency fund.** Going into more debt to cover something unexpected turns an <u>emergency</u> into a <u>crisis</u>.

Start Choosing

- **To put yourself in a position where you don't care about your bank's overdraft policies and fees – because the issue never comes up for you.** You don't live life that close to the edge.

- **The first step to financial freedom and independence.** There is (and absolutely should be) a sense of pride that comes from being able to handle what life throws at you without resorting to borrowing money (from the bank or anyone else).

5

STEP TWO - PAY OFF ALL DEBT EXCEPT THE HOUSE USING THE DEBT SNOWBALL (OR SOME VARIATION THEREOF).

We have arrived at the moment of truth. You are motivated. You are making intentional financial decisions. You have made a monthly budget or two (with some reasonable adjustments because you're new at this) and are living by that budget. Your starter emergency fund is in place. <u>It's time to punch that debt in the mouth! Let's go!</u>

Ramsey advises using the "debt snowball" method to pay off your debts. In the debt snowball, you list your debts from smallest to largest (regardless of interest rate) and pay them off in the order listed. Once that first, smallest debt is gone, you take everything you were paying on that debt and apply it to the next smallest debt. You repeat the process until all your debts are gone. <u>While this may not make the most sense from a pure math standpoint, the theory is that the psychological "wins" of crossing creditor after creditor off your list gives you the necessary excitement and momentum to keep going – like a snowball rolling down a hill</u>. Ramsey (and other proponents of the debt snowball) argue that this momentum is more important than the (often relatively small) interest rate savings that come from the "debt avalanche."

In the debt avalanche, you list your debts from highest to lowest interest rate, and you tackle the highest interest debt first. Once you clear that first debt, you take what you were paying on that loan and apply it to the one with the next highest interest rate. Assuming that what you pay towards your debt each month remains the same either way, the debt avalanche will allow you to pay the least interest during your debt-free journey – which should enable you to get to the end the quickest. The (potential) problem is the lack of momentum that comes from the victory of knocking out debt after debt. Your highest-interest debt will cost the most in interest to knock out – and if those high-interest debts have large balances, it may be quite some time until you can kick a creditor to the curb.

Let's say you are at the beginning of Step Two, and you have the following debts:

- Debt 1: Car Loan ($25,000 at 10% interest)
- Debt 2: Credit Card ($5,000 at 20% interest)
- Debt 3: Medical Debt ($10,000 at 5% interest)
- Debt 4: Student Loan ($20,000 at 8% interest)

Debt Snowball

The Debt Snowball Method would have you attack these debts in the following order:

1) Credit Card ($5,000 at 20% interest)
2) Medical Debt ($10,000 at 5% interest)
3) Student Loan ($20,000 at 8% interest)
4) Car Loan ($25,000 at 10% interest)

Debt Avalanche

The Debt Avalanche Method would have you go at your debts

in this order:

1) Credit Card ($5,000 at 20% interest)
2) Car Loan ($25,000 at 10% interest)
3) Student Loan ($20,000 at 8% interest)
4) Medical Debt ($10,000 at 5% interest)

We did a bit of a hybrid. We knocked out the smallest debts (for our phones and furniture) first – even though they were all interest-free. We were following the debt snowball method. However, what we did next broke from the snowball orthodoxy. We had to borrow about $14,000 to buy our replacement 2011 van. The loan itself was not the issue – the $14,000 loan (in part) facilitated getting us out of the $40,000 loan for our 2018 van. The issue was that we borrowed that $14,000 from my parents. I am not a fan of borrower/lender relationships among family members. Family gatherings, holidays, birthdays, etc., are at least a bit awkward when a family member is also your debtor or creditor. I mean, what birthday gift is appropriate when you owe dad money? Regardless of what you spend, your old man is likely thinking, "Save your money and pay me back already!"

My parents <u>never did anything</u> to make us feel awkward – but we felt awkward nonetheless. We wanted to eliminate the awkwardness as soon as possible. So, even though the $14,000 was one of our largest individual debts (we could break down our student loan debt into several much smaller individual loans that we could knock out one by one) and even though it had no interest (thanks, mom and dad!), we chose to pay it off first. We followed neither the debt snowball nor the debt avalanche method in making this choice. This debt would have been dead last in the debt avalanche and almost last in the debt snowball. However, paying it first aligned best with our values and priorities. Getting my parents paid was more important than the psychological gains of crossing off other creditors, and it was infinitely more important than saving a few bucks in interest. The deviation was intentional

– and I have no issue with just about any deviation from the general plan that is intentional and keeps you moving towards the ultimate goal.

With that exception, we generally stuck to the debt snowball method of paying off the smallest debts first and rolling up those debt payments as we went. Paying off debt after debt after debt just got more exciting – almost addictive – as we moved through the process. Mr. Ramsey always says personal finance is "80% behavior and only 20% head knowledge," which was 100% true for us. We just caught fire! I started taking every chance I could to talk to people about our financial epiphany, the process of becoming debt-free, how it was going for us, and why everyone should do what we were doing. Sometimes, I would catch myself ranting and force myself to take a breath and calm down. Other times, I would become aware that my eyes were as wide as saucers, and I was coming off as a bit unhinged. But I couldn't help it! I had had my "sick and tired of being sick and tired" moment! I was on the path to financial freedom – and it felt amazing! I wanted to help others get that feeling and get on the same path – I still do! That's why I decided to write this book!

Because of our experience with it and because I believe the psychological momentum of eliminating debt after debt is worth more than the interest savings, I prefer the debt snowball method and recommend it as a rule of thumb. <u>However, your method (debt snowball, debt avalanche, hybrid) is not as important as staying motivated throughout the journey</u>. When we got going, we were (and still are) what the Ramsey folks call "Gazelle Intense." Gazelle Intensity refers to the mindset of running from your debt with the same intensity a gazelle has as it runs from a cheetah. The gazelle runs with some serious purpose because its life depends upon it. Similarly, your debt is chasing you; if you don't run away from it like your life depends on it, it will take you down. I love that analogy. However, it will only motivate us to go so far (or so fast).

The cheetah in this scenario is pretty intense as well! It needs to eat to survive! <u>We need to be just as fierce as the cheetah in terms of what we are running towards</u>. What are you chasing – and maybe more importantly – why are you chasing it? Getting out of debt and building wealth just for the sake of doing it won't likely provide you with the fuel you need to get there. Why do you want to get out of debt? Why do you want to build wealth? What is the point? For my wife and me, it is because we want to help our kids make it through school without incurring the debt that we did. We don't want to stress about (or go into debt) paying for the weddings of our two daughters. We want to retire when we are young enough to enjoy our future grandchildren, serve full-time missions for our church, enjoy traveling, and help care for our parents as they age. In a word, we are running towards freedom. That freedom is our "why." Maybe you want to travel the world, or perhaps you want to find that one special place and never have to leave. Maybe you want the time and freedom to write that book or start that business. Whatever it is, I encourage you to focus on that – at least as much as you focus on the big, nasty, hairy debt chasing you.

Okay, now you are gazelle (and cheetah) intense. You have nailed down "why" you are on your journey. Let's dive a bit more into "how" you are going to dig yourself out of debt (beyond doing a monthly budget and living by it). Let's start with some Step Two Frequently Asked Questions:

1) **I've heard Dave Ramsey talk about only eating "beans and rice, and rice and beans" to save money while getting out of debt – is he serious (and do you agree with him)?** Only eating beans and rice is not his literal advice (as it would probably result in serious health problems). He is trying to convey that you can create some real margin in your budget by paying freaking attention to what you spend on food (both in the grocery store and in restaurants) each month. I completely agree. Shop the

grocery store ads, buy the store brand instead of the name brand, buy in bulk (when it makes sense and you won't end up wasting what you buy), trade in beef for chicken or pork, get creative with ramen, learn to enjoy tuna fish sandwiches, and actually plan your meals instead of flying by the seat of your pants. Do these things, and your grocery savings will be insane!

However, the most significant savings will come from paying freaking attention to what you spend at restaurants. Ramsey says that during Step Two, "the only time you should see the inside of a restaurant is if you're working there[19]." Do I agree? Not 100%. <u>What you should never do while you're paying off your debt is pay for a food delivery service. You should consider working for DoorDash or Uber Eats while trying to get out of debt. You should not use their services</u>. According to the New York Times, using a food delivery app can increase the cost of your meal by as much as 91%[20]! When it comes to restaurants, I know you will hit McDonald's (or Taco Bell or Subway) occasionally. I'm cool with that – but keep it to fast food joints where you can get out for under $10 per person. You will be able to spend up to $20 a head (including tip) at Chili's or Applebee's (or somewhere nicer) soon – but not during Step Two. <u>As a rule of thumb, your monthly restaurant budget should not exceed 10% of your grocery budget while paying off your debt</u>. For example, while we were in Step Two, our monthly grocery budget was usually $900, and our restaurant budget was $90 (for a family of five).

2) **I have money saved in a 401k or IRA. Should I cash that out and use it towards my debt?** Nope. Why? One word:

---

[19] https://twitter.com/DaveRamsey/status/1229425772546449409
[20] https://www.nytimes.com/2020/02/26/technology/personaltech/ubereats-doordash-postmates-grubhub-review.html

taxes. If you are under age 59 ½, you will pay income taxes and a 10% early withdrawal penalty on what you take out. This means you could pay almost 50% of what you take out in taxes. <u>I want you to pay off your debt – not to help the federal government pay off theirs (as if that would ever happen)</u>. There are better ways to get through Baby Step Two than raiding what you have in your retirement.

3) **I really like my car – do I have to sell it?** Not necessarily. There are two rules of thumb here:

- **You should not have more than 50% of your annual household income tied up in things with wheels or motors (cars, trucks, boats, ATVs, etc.).** For example, if you have $40,000 worth of vehicles (or vehicle debt) and a household income of $75,000, it's time to make some changes. Our situation back in August 2019 did not violate this rule of thumb. Our $47,000 vehicle debt was less than 50% of our household income. However …

- **(If you love it) you can keep your vehicle (and your debt for it) if you can be entirely out of non-mortgage debt within two years**. This is where we knew we had a problem. We estimated getting out of debt would take 3 to 4 years. Because of this, we needed to sell the 2018 van and get a jumpstart on attacking our debt. The $17,000 in debt we eliminated and the $400+ in monthly cash flow we created by moving down in vehicle gave us the early momentum we needed to tackle our debt.

Also, please realize that your vehicles are typically the most significant purchases you will make on assets that go down in value. Because of this, they are also the purchases that steal the largest proportion of your wealth. The average new vehicle depreciates 40% over the first five years[21]. The average car loan is 72 months[22]. So, on average, when you finance a $50,000 car (with no down payment), after five years, you will have:

- Made 60 monthly payments of about $842/month (assuming an interest rate of 6.58% - which is the average new car interest rate as of the first quarter of 2023[23]);

- Paid $50,520 already ($842 x 60 months) and still have $10,104 left to go ($842 x 12 months); and

- A vehicle that is worth $30,000.

This means you took $50,520 and turned it into $30,000 – and you still owe an additional $10,000+ for the privilege. Even if you paid $50,000 in cash for the car, you would have taken $50,000 and turned it into $30,000. Another way to accomplish the same thing in the same timeframe would be to go into your backyard on the first day of each month for the next 60 months with $333 in your pocket. Take a lighter with you. Once you are a safe distance from your home, take the cash out of one pocket and the lighter out of the other. Carefully place the money on the ground – <u>and light it on fire</u>.

On the other hand, if you had paid cash for a $10,000 car and invested the remaining $40,000 at $667/month for 60 months at an 8% annual return, you'd have a car worth $6,000, and your investments would be worth about $49,000. So, you would have taken $50,000 and turned it into

---

[21] https://www.lendingtree.com/auto/how-much-do-new-cars-depreciate/
[22] https://www.investopedia.com/how-long-are-car-loans-7498900
[23] https://www.nerdwallet.com/article/loans/auto-loans/average-car-loan-interest-rates-by-credit-score

$55,000.

Please don't misunderstand me – I want you to have a nice car! I plan to have one or two of them myself soon! But I don't want the car to have you. This means waiting until you can pay cash and waiting until the $25,000 difference after five years is insignificant to your overall net worth. <u>There is no situation under which I would advise you to finance or lease a depreciating asset like a personal vehicle. Always pay cash (or perhaps finance it to get a better deal and pay it off immediately)!</u>

4) **Can I take a vacation?** A full-blown vacation where you jump on a plane or a cruise ship and spend thousands of dollars? Sorry, but nope! However, this doesn't mean you don't need a break. Taking a few days off can absolutely be beneficial during Step Two. But this can't be a situation where you take one step forward and two steps back. <u>Going into more debt for a vacation is not an option</u>. We visited Grandma and Grandpa a lot during Step Two. We also took a couple of trips to National Parks (Zion and Bryce Canyon are less than two hours away). We left the kids with Grandma for one night and stayed in Park City (within driving distance) for our anniversary. Here are some ideas:

- **Visit a National Park or historical site.**
- **Stay with family** (unless the idea of doing so is the exact opposite of a vacation for you).
- **Go camping** (like in an actual tent).
- **Keep it short.** Make it a three or four-day weekend instead of two weeks gallivanting through Europe.
- **Keep it local.** It doesn't have to be far away to be awesome.
- **Plan ahead.** Booking well in advance can yield incredible savings.

- **Go when other people aren't.** Think the beach when it's not all that warm or ski towns when the snow is gone.
- **Find a grocery store** (I promise they have them wherever you're headed) and make some of your own meals. This works especially well for lunches.
- **Understand that you are not making a long-term commitment to the hotel.** Consider how much time you will spend in the room (i.e., not much) and make your booking decisions accordingly. You will survive a night or two at the Econolodge or Motel 6. I promise!
- **A cheap airfare or hotel deal (in and of itself) is not a reason to take a vacation.** If you spend $1,000 instead of the $1,500 retail price on a trip you didn't need to take, you didn't save $500. You spent $1,000 you shouldn't have spent.

5) **Should I sell my house to pay off debt?** This question allows me to offer an attorney's favorite answer – it depends! It depends on whether you are "house-poor." <u>If your mortgage payment exceeds 25% of your monthly take-home pay, you are house-poor</u>. Don't shoot the messenger – but you bought too much house. Just because a bank will loan you the money doesn't mean you should take it. If you are house-poor, you need to explore the possibility of selling your home and using the profits to pay off (or at least pay down) your debt. Obviously, there are logistical and emotional factors to consider when making this decision. However, from a purely economic standpoint, here is what to look at:

- **Will you make a profit if you sell?** Ideally, your home should be worth more than you paid for it and more than you owe on it – hopefully, substantially more. This may not be an ideal time to sell if it isn't.

- **What will you pay in taxes?** If you own the property personally (or in the name of a typical living trust) and have lived in the property as your primary residence for at least two of the previous five years, Section 121 of the tax code says the first $250,000 of profit on the sale of the home is tax-free if you are single[24]. The exemption doubles to $500,000 for married taxpayers[25]. This is known as the "Sale of Home Exemption."

    Any gain above those exemptions (I'm looking at you, California) will be subject to long-term capital gains tax. Depending on your income, that tax rate will typically be 15% or 20% at the federal level. In most cases, you will also owe state-level taxes on that part of the gain. If you've lived in the home for more than a year but less than two, the entire gain will be subject to tax at the long-term capital gains rates. If you've lived there less than a year, you'll pay taxes on all the profit at short-term capital gains rates. Those rates are the same as ordinary income tax rates, which are as high as 37% at the federal level - depending on your income. If federal and state taxes will eat up 40% or more of your profit from a sale, then it makes sense to wait until you've lived in the home for at least a year before you sell. It can make even more sense to wait until you've lived in the home for at least two years so you can claim the Sale of Home Exemption on the first $250,000 or $500,000 of gain.

- **Can you find a suitable place to rent that is no more expensive than your mortgage?** I realize that "suitable" is a loaded word in this context. You need to be willing to make sacrifices, but if rents have skyrocketed where you live, you may need to consider

---

[24] 26 U.S.C. § 121(a)
[25] 26 U.S.C. § 121(b)

relocating.

Okay, we've tackled several FAQs about Step Two I get from clients and other people. But, easily, the most common question people ask is, "Is it okay to use my credit cards?" Mr. Ramsey says no. Full stop. End of sentence. My answer is also no – if you are going to carry a balance. Doing that would be counterproductive at best. Okay, but what if I pay off the balance every month? The Ramsey answer is still "no." Why? Well, it's a bit like telling a recovering alcoholic it's okay to have a glass of wine with dinner occasionally. It might be just fine. But then again, it may end up with that recovering alcoholic waking up under a freeway overpass in Vegas after a three-day bender trying to figure out where exactly he is and just how the hell he's going to get home. Using a credit card allows you to take on debt and fall off the financial wagon because you needed (or wanted) it "just this once." I'd be willing to bet that a massive chunk of the 40% of credit card users who carry debt from month to month[26] had every intention of paying off their balance every cycle – but (for one reason or another) it didn't happen. Then, if you don't watch out, you end up like the 15% of Americans who have been in credit card debt for at least 15 years[27].

The other reason credit cards can be dangerous is that they make it easier to spend money. A recent study found that the average credit card transaction is $57, whereas the average cash transaction is $22[28]. There are several reasons why this is true, but it is primarily because credit cards decrease the "friction" associated with spending money. When you use a credit card, you hand the cashier your plastic, they run the card, and they hand the plastic back to you – along with the items you've purchased. You can then check your bank account balance on your phone, and it

---

[26] https://www.lendingtree.com/credit-cards/credit-card-debt-statistics/
[27] https://inside1031.com/credit-card-debt-2021/
[28] https://upgradedpoints.com/credit-cards/credit-spending-facts-statistics/

will be the same as before the transaction. You know better, but somewhere in the primitive part of your brain, it feels like you got something for nothing. The other end of the friction spectrum would be using cash – especially if you don't have any. There is a ton of friction there. To make that same purchase, you'd have to locate a nearby ATM or bank, drive there, withdraw the cash, and then drive to the store. Once you enter the store and select your item(s), you head to the cashier. You'll then hand the cashier Messrs. Franklin, Jackson, Hamilton, Lincoln, and Washington, and the cashier will give you your item(s). Those dead presidents aren't coming back. There is no feeling of "something for nothing" here. Spending that money was a chore (and maybe one you don't want to repeat).

Somewhere in the middle of the friction spectrum is the debit card. The debit card has a Visa or MasterCard symbol, so you can use it like a credit card. This removes much of the friction of obtaining, organizing, and safeguarding cash. However, the debit card is tied to your bank account – so when you check your bank account after using a debit card, you will find a dent in that account – the balance will be lower. This gives you a real-time gauge of where you stand – unlike the multiple steps involved in checking your credit card balance against your bank account balance and making sure you will have enough to pay off the credit card when it comes due at the end of the month.

The other side argues that when you use a credit card that offers miles/points/cash back and pay off your credit card balance each month, you pay nothing in interest and benefit from those miles/points/cash back. So, according to these folks, it's just plain stupid to use a debit card instead of a rewards or cash-back credit card. If everything else is equal, this argument holds water. However, I do have some real-world experience here. Before we started this journey in 2019, our family almost exclusively used a Costco Visa card for our expenses. The Costco card offered 1%-3% cash back, depending on where we used it. We paid it off every month, and we'd get about $1,000 back from Costco every February. Once we started making intentional financial decisions, we switched over and started using our debit card almost exclusively. Our experience (which no doubt was also greatly influenced by the fact that we started following Ramsey and doing a monthly budget) is that we spent significantly less each month using a debit card than a credit card. We certainly saved more than the $80-$85 per month we earned in cash back.

However, please notice I said we moved <u>almost</u> exclusively to the debit card. We had a handful of automatic monthly payments (for utilities, etc.) tied to our credit card. These automatic payments were for non-discretionary expenses. Therefore, because the amount of "friction" in these transactions was essentially irrelevant (and because changing the card was a bit of a pain), we left these automatic payments on our Costco credit card throughout our debt-free journey. This allowed us to continue receiving cash back (although on a much smaller scale) while increasing the friction in spending money – all of which allowed us to get out of debt quicker than otherwise may have been the case.

Here are my bottom-line thoughts on credit cards:

- **Once you pay off your cards, you never, ever, EVER carry a balance again!**

- **Avoid using credit cards during Steps One through Three.** You can use them for automatic payments (like we did), but I don't want them sitting in your wallet or purse where they can tempt you to use them to pay for things you don't need and can't afford. Mr. Ramsey would have you cut them up. At the very least, put them in a location where getting to them will be physically difficult. Lock them in a safe that only a trusted person has access to. Have your kids devise an incredibly complex scavenger hunt you will have to unravel to find them – something!

- **After you have paid off all your debts except your house and have saved an emergency fund equal to 3-6 months of expenses (i.e., you've completed Step Three), I am going to depart from Ramsey a bit. At that point, I am open to using a cashback or rewards credit card for expenses and paying it off every month – as long as:**

    1. It is within the framework of a zero-based budget;

    2. You track your expenses/purchases throughout the month in the same way you would with cash or debit card purchases; and

    3. You think you are disciplined enough to live with the financial equivalent of a loaded weapon in your wallet. I can't stress this enough – credit cards are freaking dangerous. Just like firearms, when not used properly, they **will** inflict unintended injury (of the financial type). But, when used correctly, they can provide some advantages. You must decide for yourself and your family if the risks (of overspending, incurring debt, and paying interest) are worth the rewards (cash back, points, miles, etc.). Please also know that this decision can (and should be) revisited and reevaluated as you progress. <u>What do we do? For now, we choose to live without them, except for the "fixed" expenses I explained above.</u>

- **You are not "unsophisticated," "stupid," or "missing out" if you go through the analysis above and decide you want to live a life without credit cards.** You are choosing the financial equivalent of not keeping a loaded gun in the house. <u>Do not listen to anyone who tells you otherwise!</u> And remember, no wealthy person has ever said, "My key to building wealth was credit card rewards!"

Another question I get from people going through Step Two is how to deal with debts that could be forgiven or have no interest. I have some experience with this. When Covid hit in March 2020, and Joe Biden won the presidency in November 2020, we had to think about this. Our student loans had no interest, and "Grandpa Joe" ran on a platform that included at least some version of student loan forgiveness. One school of thought would have been to stop our student loan payments entirely and start investing the funds earmarked for repaying the debt. The other end of the spectrum would have been to continue the debt snowball with no variation. We took a bit of a middle road. We moved the federal student loans that could be subject to debt forgiveness to the end of the snowball and paid off the remaining private student loans first. However, we never paused our student loan payments. If some form of debt forgiveness came during the ordinary course of paying our loans, that would be awesome (I've never been one to turn down free money). However, we were not interested in putting our lives on hold while waiting for someone else (especially the government) to fix our problems.

Student loan relief never came for us while we were paying off our loans. We made our last student loan payment in March 2022. As it turned out, President Biden did propose to cancel $10,000-$20,000 in student debt in August 2022. However, we don't regret the way we did it. A priceless sense of peace came from paying off our debt as soon as possible – not to mention the satisfaction of being able to say that we took care of our obligations. We didn't wait around for Uncle Sam to save us. We handled those debts without relying on a government handout. So, when the Supreme Court struck down Biden's student debt forgiveness plan in June 2023 – the outcome was a non-factor in our house. I smirked a bit and moved on with my day.

Don't count on anyone else to fix your problems. This is even truer if you are relying on the government to do it. <u>Your debt is your problem. Take some ownership of your life and go fix the</u>

problem! This doesn't mean you can't strategically place forgivable debts at the end of your snowball. But don't play games when it comes time to pay them. Get them paid immediately. Don't delay the peace of living debt-free by a single day!

Step Two is a slog. There will be times when you will feel like it will never end – that you will be in debt forever, so you might as well give up. I can tell you from experience that this isn't true. When you feel like that, I want you to let yourself start dreaming (maybe even salivating) about how life will look when you don't have any more payments. Where will you go? What will you drive? What sort of legacy will you leave for your family? As you allow yourself to ponder these questions, your motivation will return. You will want to do whatever it takes to leave Step Two behind as quickly as possible.

We have talked a lot about playing defense in this game by reducing your expenses, but you will also want to play offense by increasing your income. You may be able to increase your hours at work, or it may be time for that "side hustle." Having a side hustle is a great way to increase the size of the shovel you will use to dig yourself out of your hole of debt. Here are some fantastic side hustle ideas[29] [30]:

- Drive for Lyft or Uber
- Deliver food (DoorDash, Grubhub, etc.)
- Deliver groceries
- Rent out a spare room on Airbnb
- Rent out your car
- Become an online coach
- Start a YouTube channel
- Start a photography business

---

[29] https://time.com/nextadvisor/financial-independence/best-side-hustles/
[30] https://www.ramseysolutions.com/saving/side-hustle-ideas

- Join a focus group or take surveys
- Tutor or teach English online
- Resell clothing that is already in your closet
- Freelance as a writer, editor, graphic designer, or voice-over artist
- Sell products you create on Etsy
- Do odd jobs and tasks for others on sites like TaskRabbit or Handy
- Teach music lessons
- Clean houses
- Babysit
- Walk dogs or pet sit
- Become a user tester
- Sell baked goods
- Lease out your garage or yard space for storage
- Referee youth sports
- Do yard work
- Deliver packages with Amazon Flex
- Write an adorable children's book for Halloween about why witches always wear black. <u>Oh wait – I already took that one</u>[31]!

Two points of caution when it comes to starting a business or side hustle while you are still in Step Two:

1) **Beware of any business that requires a large upfront cash outlay.** Say it with me – <u>"I will not borrow any money to start a side hustle."</u> You can get started on most of the ideas in the list above with little or nothing out of pocket. Going into more debt to start a side hustle would be beyond foolish. Be especially wary of anyone trying to sell you an expensive "package" or "training" to create a side hustle.

---

[31] https://whydowitcheswearblack.com/

2) **(Unless it really sucks) don't quit your day job.** In most cases, these side hustles will not be as lucrative or steady as your 8-5 grind. Unless you are doing better per hour with the side hustle, your current job has no room for growth, and you are confident you can get as many hours in the side hustle as you get with the 8-5, the side hustle should be an additional source of income – not the only source.

In most side hustles, there is no employer to issue you a W-2, withhold taxes, and pay benefits. <u>Guess what? Whether you realize it or not, that makes you a small business owner! Owning your own business is a great way to increase your income and opens up incredible opportunities to decrease one of the most significant hidden expenses in your life – taxes[32]</u>! Helping business owners save on taxes is my day job! Let's look at just a few of the tax benefits small business owners can take advantage of:

1) **You can pay your children with pre-tax dollars[33]**. Get your kids involved in your side hustle! Maybe they can do your social media marketing or help with bookkeeping. Have them clean the room you are renting on Airbnb between renters. Find something legitimate and valuable for them to do for your business, pay them a reasonable amount for that work, have a written log (electronic is fine) of what they did and when, and move the corresponding amount to their personal bank account. When you do this, the amount you pay your kids is an "ordinary and necessary" business expense, which means you won't pay taxes on it. Also, in 2023, every American has a "Standard Deduction" of $13,850. This means no one (including your kids) pays federal taxes on the first $13,850 they make this year – so (assuming they make less than $13,850) your kids won't pay

---

[32] https://markjkohler.com/how-a-small-business-saves-taxes-and-builds-true-wealth/
[33] https://markjkohler.com/how-to-pay-your-kids-in-your-business/

taxes on it either. <u>Have the kids use that money to pay school/sports/extra-curricular fees, to go to the movies, or for that new video game they've been dying for – you know, the stuff you were going to pay for anyway</u>. The only difference is now, instead of getting paid, paying taxes, and then paying for these things, you are paying for them with money that was never taxed.

<u>Please don't get carried away here.</u> Your toddler may be adorable, but paying them $2,500 for a two-hour photo session so you could get some photos to put on your website isn't going to fly (unless you can show that your toddler regularly makes a $1,250/hour modeling fee). **<u>A saying applies here (and with most tax savings strategies). Pigs get fat – hogs get slaughtered. Don't be a hog!</u>**

2) **You can write off travel expenses**[34]. When you travel for business, your airfare, hotel/Airbnb, rental cars, Uber/Lyft fees, tolls, parking fees, etc., are all write-offs. Of course, your vacation is not business travel if it doesn't have a business purpose. But what if it was for your company's annual meeting? Or for training or education related to your business? Or to visit a client or vendor? <u>When you have your own business, opportunities abound for you to turn your travel into a business expense</u>. Remember that not every penny you spend during the trip will likely be eligible for a write-off when you combine business with pleasure. However, without a side hustle, nothing would be.

3) **You can write off your health insurance premiums**[35]. Some employers provide (and pay for) health insurance for their employees – but many don't. This is a huge potential

---

[34] https://markjkohler.com/how-to-write-off-your-travel-expenses/
[35] https://markjkohler.com/how-to-write-off-health-insurance-in-my-business/

savings if you are among the millions who purchase their own health insurance (either on an exchange or directly from a private company)! The average monthly premium for a 40-year-old on a "Silver" plan is $560. That's almost $7,000 per year. When employees pay health insurance premiums, they do so with after-tax dollars. Not so for small business owners. <u>Every dollar of health insurance premiums a business owner pays is a business expense</u>. This deduction could save you thousands in taxes every year!

Ok. You are working through Step Two. Your budget is dialed in – allowing you to find money you didn't even know you had. Maybe you've picked up a side hustle to increase income and save on taxes. You're knocking out debts left and right! What could possibly go wrong? I can think of a few things:

- **You could run into a significant, unexpected expense.** This happened to us. We were on track to be debt-free in February 2022. Then, in early January, my wife called me at work to tell me she was stranded on the side of the road near our home. Our van (which had worked beautifully for almost two-and-a-half years) would not move. We took it into the shop, and they informed us that the transmission was shot. We needed a new one. Supply chain issues meant we wouldn't get one for 4-8 weeks. The cost to obtain the new transmission and install it was $7,500. We had the $7,500 available (it was earmarked to pay down debt, but now we needed it for transportation). We felt that paying cash for a new van didn't make sense because $7,500 would likely only get us a vehicle where we might be paying for a transmission soon anyway.

    We had a choice to make. We could either pay $7,500 for a new transmission or use the $7,500 as a down payment on a new $15,000-$20,000 van. However, we had made our choice two-and-a-half years earlier. Taking on more debt wasn't an option. Our (incredible) neighbors let us borrow their extra car for more than a month, and when our van was ready, I walked into the dealership (where it was being repaired) and stroked them a check for $7,500. Was it weird writing a check for that much at a dealership and not walking out with a new vehicle? Yes, it was – but it was the right choice. <u>Don't use an unexpected expense as an excuse to incur more debt. There is almost always a way to proceed that doesn't include debt</u>.

- **You could decide to consolidate your debt.** Wait, debt consolidation is a bad thing? Not necessarily, <u>but let's make sure we are crystal clear – taking out a second mortgage, HELOC, or debt consolidation loan to eliminate credit card or car debt does not mean you have paid off anything</u>! It can feel that way – "Honey, we did it! The credit card debt is gone!" But it is a false sense of security/accomplishment. Why? Because:

    - <u>All you've done is move the debt from one place to another</u>. Consolidating your debt is not the same as paying it off. It's still there. It's just somewhere else. Your net worth has not changed!

    - <u>If you consolidate your debt, then you must commit to avoiding the debt "tools" that got you into the mess in the first place</u>. If you go right back to using that credit card to pay for a nice dinner or buying that new bedroom set on store credit, then you are the personification of Proverbs 26:11: "As a dog returns to its vomit, so a fool repeats his folly." It may be time for some "plastic surgery" (cutting up the credit cards). The definition of insanity is doing the same thing over and over again and expecting a different result. Using the same credit card or line of credit you just eliminated with the consolidation loan would be insane.

- <u>Debt consolidation can help with the math of getting out of debt (because the overall interest rate is lower than the interest rates on the debt you are consolidating – or at least it should be!), but it can actually hurt when it comes to the psychology of getting out of debt</u>. The psychology of the debt snowball is simple and brilliant. The satisfaction of kicking a creditor to the curb, crossing them off your list, and turning around to fist-bump your family and friends is real – I know from experience! Getting that first win gives you some serious motivation to get another one and another one until all your debt is gone. <u>You don't get those little wins with one giant debt consolidation loan</u>. Yes, you can celebrate as the balance on that loan gets smaller, but the satisfaction of moving from $50,000 in debt to $40,000 in debt just isn't the same as paying off your car and screaming, "I will never send another penny to those blankety-blanks at Ford Motor Credit again!" Many people get discouraged or overwhelmed without these small victories and simply give up.

<u>Debt consolidation is not always the answer. My advice would be not to consolidate your debt unless</u>:

1. The difference in the interest rates is more than 5%, and
2. You won't be able to eliminate all your non-mortgage debt in less than two years.

In most cases, the interest rate on your debt is not the problem. Being honest about your finances and motivated and willing to make the necessary sacrifices to eliminate your debt and obtain financial freedom is.

Let's do the math. Let's say you have $25,000 in debt spread across multiple lenders, and the average interest rate is 10%.

Let's also assume you are ready to buckle down and are willing and able to pay $1,500/month to tackle that debt. In that scenario, you would pay off the debt in <u>18 months – while paying a total of $2,063.51 in interest</u>. If, instead, you get a debt consolidation loan that reduces the interest rate on those same loans to 6%, and you make the same monthly payment of $1,500, you would pay off the loan in, wait for it … <u>the same 18 months while paying a total of $1,183.65 in interest</u>.

The difference in the interest paid is $880. Over 18 months, that is $49/month. <u>$49 per month is not keeping you from paying off your debt. Your high interest rate is not keeping you from paying off your debt. Your lifestyle choices are.</u> Consolidating your debt won't change the fact that your daily spending decisions are causing you to live beyond your means. If you aren't willing to change your lifestyle and make intentional financial decisions, your debt consolidation won't mean a thing.

- **You could worry too much about what other people think.** Americans have a record $1.031 trillion in credit card debt[36], $1.56 trillion in auto debt[37], and $1.77 trillion in student loan debt[38]. The federal government is about $32 trillion in debt (just over $98,000 for every person in the country)[39]. <u>So, when you choose to go without things you can "afford" to live a debt-free life, people will think you are weird – because you are</u>. Debt is so ingrained in our culture that we genuinely believe Visa is "everywhere we want to be," and when Capital One asks us "what's in our wallet," we are proud to answer, "the instruments of financial servitude you sold me!" Even though an authority no less

---

[36] https://www.lendingtree.com/credit-cards/credit-card-debt-statistics/
[37] https://www.lendingtree.com/auto/debt-statistics/
[38] https://www.lendingtree.com/student/student-loan-debt-statistics/
[39] https://www.pgpf.org/national-debt-clock

than the Bible says, "the borrower is servant to the lender[40]," we worship at the altar of the almighty credit score and wonder how we would ever obtain the things we want and need without taking out a loan.

When you commit to this process, you are going against the grain. <u>People will not only think you're nuts – some of them will be mad at you</u>. They'll be angry because you'll stop going where they go, buying what they buy, and living as they live. They will start projecting their feelings onto you. They will accuse you of thinking you are better than them. In many ways, debt is an addiction. When addicts decide to leave and get help, it is common for the community of addicts they left behind to be resentful – not happy. You will have people in your life that feel that way. You may lose some friends. At the very least, there will be some people you will need to avoid for a while.

- **You could get caught in the trap of "keeping up with the Joneses."** The concept of wanting to have what someone else has is nothing new. It's been around as long as humans have. The phrase "keeping up with the Joneses" comes from a comic strip of the same name that ran from 1913-40[41]. However, our lives have never been on display for the world to see in the way they have since the advent of social media. Every event (special or otherwise), vacation, major purchase, and sometimes, meal is documented. However, our social media profiles rarely accurately portray our lives. Sure, we might post a photo of our family stranded at the airport on the way to Disneyworld with sad face emojis. But we do it because we are fishing for sympathetic responses (and we want people to know we are going to Disneyworld). We fail to mention that we can't seem to get

---

[40] Proverbs 22:7
[41] https://en.wikipedia.org/wiki/Keeping_up_with_the_Joneses

through to the 14-year-old who won't look up from his phone, and that we are hoping to connect with our spouse on this trip because we've felt alone for a really long time. Married couples routinely profess their undying love for each other on Instagram, only to file for divorce weeks later.

In the age of social media, keeping up with the Joneses is a bigger problem than ever. Instead of comparing ourselves to our neighbors when we drive past their houses and see that new Mercedes or boat in the driveway, we do it every time we look at our phones (which we do dozens of times each day). That nagging feeling that you aren't good enough (or doing enough) never really goes away if you're constantly checking your feed. This can be especially true when sacrificing to pay off your debt. Your posts won't be filled with exotic vacation photos, new vehicles, or beautiful plates of food from expensive restaurants – your "friends'" posts will. You need to know that – and be okay with it. If you aren't, you won't get very far.

- **You could buy into the culture of entitlement that pervades our modern society.** The same people who resent you for choosing to sacrifice in the short term to experience financial freedom will tell you that you "deserve" to take that expensive vacation or buy that pricey new car. We deserve what we earn, and when we borrow money to obtain things we haven't earned, we trade a tomorrow filled with peace, contentment, and fulfillment for some temporary pleasure (clothes, a nice dinner out, a vacation, a car) today. When you live in the cycle of debt, you are always paying (with interest) for things you already did and stuff you already bought. You are constantly looking back. When you choose to live debt-free, you are continually saving (with interest) for what you will do or buy next. You are always looking forward – to the future. <u>Choose to focus on the future!</u>

When you focus on the future, you will <u>intentionally</u> sacrifice some things you want to do or buy today. Sometimes, that will be a bummer – I understand that. I have experienced it. However, I steadfastly believe this: "Anyone who imagines that bliss is normal is going to waste a lot of time running around shouting that he's been robbed. Most putts don't drop. Most beef is tough. Most children grow up to be just people. Most successful marriages require a high degree of mutual toleration. Most jobs are more often dull than otherwise. Life is like an old-time rail journey – delays, sidetracks, smoke, dust, cinders, and jolts, interspersed only occasionally by beautiful vistas and thrilling bursts of speed. The trick is to thank the Lord for letting you have the ride.[42]"

Stop Choosing

- **To believe that debt is the only way to get the things you want.** Saving up and paying cash gives the control back to you and shifts the power of interest in your favor.

- **To make banks and credit card companies rich.** Not to pick on Chase, but one of their credit cards is the *Chase Freedom Unlimited* card. It is difficult for me to adequately express how much I hate that name. The *Freedom Unlimited* card has a 0% APR for 15 months. Okay, great – but after that, the APR jumps to a variable rate of 20.24%-28.99%[43]! Also (unsurprisingly), every *Freedom Unlimited* card comes with a credit limit – usually $1,000-$5,000[44]. So, to recap, with a punitive interest rate of 20-29% and a credit limit that typically doesn't exceed $5,000, the *Chase Freedom Unlimited* card is neither "free" nor "unlimited." However, it provides a sweet

---

[42] https://www.facebook.com/byuspeeches/posts/quote-of-the-week-anyone-who-imagines-that-bliss-is-normal-is-going-to-waste-a-1/10151515031965734/
[43] https://creditcards.chase.com/cash-back-credit-cards/freedom/unlimited
[44] https://www.creditdonkey.com/chase-freedom-unlimited-credit-limit.html

stream of revenue and unlimited freedom – to JPMorgan Chase Bank (not cardholders).

- **To care what other people (especially on social media) think about your finances or how you use your money.** It truly isn't their business – and their thoughts and opinions are worth what you pay for them (absolutely nothing).

- **To believe you will be in debt forever and can do nothing about it.** That is precisely how I used to think – and it simply isn't true.

- **The past.** Eliminate debt so your monthly credit card bill no longer forces you to look in the rearview at what you've already done and purchased (and how you're still paying for those things – with interest).

Start Choosing

- **Gazelle (and Cheetah) Intensity.** Let the nasty things you are running from (the crushing weight of debt and interest) and the amazing things you are running towards (a future filled with freedom and prosperity) light you up inside and guide your actions. Your friends and loved ones will wonder what has gotten into you. They (and, more importantly, you) will love the results.

- **"No."** No is not a word people use much anymore when it comes to things they (or their kids) want. Step Two is the time to learn the power of "no." Tell yourself no. Tell your kids no. It's good for them (and for you)! Do it long enough, and you'll actually start to enjoy it!
- **A side hustle.** A little extra income can go a long way and offer major tax-saving opportunities.

- **To be weird.** In today's society, delaying gratification now for a long-term goal is weird. Sacrificing to get out of debt as quickly as possible is weird. Refusing to borrow money to buy the car you really, really want now is weird. Choose to be weird because the statistics prove that normal in America sucks.

- **The future.** Focus on what you want to do next and the incredible freedom that will be yours when you are debt-free!

6

STEP THREE – SAVE 3–6 MONTHS OF EXPENSES IN A FULLY FUNDED EMERGENCY FUND

This one is pretty self-explanatory. Everyone should have a significant buffer between them and a job loss, a long-term illness or injury, or a vehicle just giving up the ghost – without being forced to go back into debt. This is the purpose of the emergency fund. The only questions are:

- **Exactly how big should this fund be?**
- **Where do I keep it?**
- **What qualifies as an "emergency"?**

So, which is it? Three months or six months (or something in between)? The rule of thumb is that the more stable your income and family situations are, the more likely you are to get away with a smaller emergency fund. Some things to think about here are:

1) **One income or two?** Dual-income households can better withstand an injury, illness, or job loss that affects only one of the breadwinners. So, a larger emergency fund probably makes sense if your family relies on only one person to bring home the bacon.

2) **Salary or Commission?** Commission or bonus-based income can be lucrative – but it also tends to be volatile. If you work on commission, a larger emergency fund will help smooth out the bumps and keep your family afloat during any rough patches.

3) **Major Health Issues?** If a member of your household has a medical condition that may require a large cash outlay to cover a bunch of trips to the doctor, surgery, or hospitalization, it is better to err on the side of a larger emergency fund.

I am our family's primary breadwinner, and my income can vary fairly significantly from month to month. As such, we decided to save five months of expenses in our emergency fund. We felt having more than three months of savings made sense, but six months felt like overkill.

Where do we stash this cash? The answer is not under the mattress (or even in a safe). People tend to gravitate to the extremes here. On one end, we have people who genuinely don't trust "the system." These folks don't want their emergency fund in a bank. They usually either want it in gold bars in their basement safe or in cryptocurrency they hold in their own personal "hardware wallet." On the other end of the spectrum, we have the people who can't stand to have any money outside of that same system. They want their money to "work for them" – so their inclination is to put the emergency fund into speculative investments.

Neither extreme is a good idea. Your emergency fund should be liquid, safe, and free from risk. <u>It is insurance</u> against all the nasty things life can throw at you – <u>it is not an investment</u>. Self-storage may feel safer, but funds in a bank or credit union are not at risk of theft, fire, flood, or forgotten passwords – and they are FDIC or NCUA insured – up to at least $250,000. They are also available to pay the landlord or car shop immediately – unlike gold bullion or the Bitcoin you keep on your thumb drive. It may also be against your nature to put the emergency fund money in the bank instead of that hot stock or ETF, but cash in the bank did not lose over 32.5% of its value in 2022 – the Nasdaq Composite Index did[45].

This doesn't mean you should settle for a savings account that pays 0.01% interest (like the one I used to have at Wells Fargo). Our emergency fund is in an online savings account at Ally Bank that the FDIC fully insures. That account currently pays 4.25% interest. Other banks pay similar (or even higher) rates. A money-market account can also be a good option – but whatever option you choose, you need to make sure you can access the funds quickly and easily.

Okay, when am I justified in spending the money in my emergency fund? To answer that question, ask yourself the following about the potential expenditure:

- **Is it unexpected?** Christmas is not an emergency!!! They have it every year! Plan for it!

- **Is it necessary?** Upgrading your car when your current one runs just fine is not an emergency!!! Save up and pay cash for the upgrade.

- **Is it urgent?** The concrete in your driveway is starting to crack pretty severely. Did you expect that? Nope. Does it need to be fixed? Yep. Can it wait three or four months while you save to pay for it? That's affirmative – which means it isn't an emergency!!!

---

[45] https://www.nasdaq.com/articles/2022-review-and-outlook

During Steps Two and Three, another important question is whether to continue investing while attacking the debt and building your emergency fund. Specifically, the question is often whether or not to continue retirement account contributions (to a 401k, IRA, etc.) while you are in that process. Mr. Ramsey advises to stop investing during Steps Two and Three[46]. He would have you stop making retirement account contributions while you pay off your debt and put together your emergency fund. The thinking behind this advice is two-fold: 1) Get rid of debt as soon as possible, giving you access to all of your income as quickly as possible to complete the remaining Steps and build wealth; and 2) This is not the time for "balance." If you try to be an investor and a rabid debt eliminator at the same time – you won't do either very well. I think this is generally good advice. I don't know about you, but when I try to do two things simultaneously, I end up not being very good at either. The Bible even says, "No man can serve two masters[47]." Because of this, we stopped making retirement account contributions when we started our debt-free journey.

However, my other financial mentor (my boss, Mark Kohler) has changed my thinking (at least a bit) on this decision. When I told him I was pausing my company 401k contributions to focus solely on eliminating debt, he appreciated why. However, our firm matches employee contributions dollar-for-dollar up to 3% of our salary and 50 cents of every dollar from 3-5% of our salary. So, if we contribute 5% of our salary to the company 401k, the firm will contribute 4%. Mark told me, "That's an 80% return on investment – it costs me money (because the firm has to make matching contributions), but you should continue contributing enough to get that match." I declined because I was obsessed with eliminating my debt as soon as possible. However, I am not opposed to folks in Steps Two and Three contributing enough to a 401k plan to maximize the match from their employer. But that's

---

[46] https://www.ramseysolutions.com/debt/pay-off-debt-before-retirement
[47] Matthew 6:24

it. Don't contribute more than that, and don't make contributions to an IRA (which aren't matched by anyone) before you are out of debt and have a fully-funded emergency fund. Saving anything more than that for retirement during Steps Two and Three is counter-productive. Don't try to do everything at once – it just doesn't work! Be intentional about getting out of debt and putting a robust buffer between you and the craziness life can dish out!

Often, people working through Steps Two and Three have already jumped into real estate investing and own a rental property with a mortgage. If this is you, you might ask yourself if you need to sell that property. To decide, first, pretend that you don't own the property. Second, estimate how much you would put into your pocket (after closing costs and taxes) if you were to sell the property. With everything in your life being the same, if you had that money sitting in front of you, would you use it to go out and buy that same property? Or would you use that money to pay off debt, finish building your emergency fund, put towards retirement, save for your kids' college education, pay down/off your home mortgage, etc.? Your answer will likely depend on the following factors:

1. **How well is the rental property performing?** The more cash flow the property provides, and the more it has appreciated (and you expect it will continue to appreciate), the more sense it makes to keep it.

2. **How much work do you have to put in?** Are you (or your property manager) over there repairing something every week? Are tenants in and out, or do you have great long-term tenants? Do you enjoy being a landlord, or is it sucking all the joy out of life?

3. **How important is it to you to eliminate debt and/or finish building your emergency fund as quickly as possible?** Selling the rental could put you on the fast track

to exiting Steps Two and Three. Is the peace of being debt-free and having 3-6 months of expenses in the bank worth more than what the rental property brings?

For me, the rental would have to perform extraordinarily well, and I would have to love being a landlord to keep it. <u>But that's because I hate debt, and I love the peace that comes with being debt-free and having a healthy emergency fund</u>. There are plenty of people who disagree with me. We will explore different schools of thought on using debt for income-producing assets in more detail in Chapter 10.

Some folks in the financial industry advocate using a home equity line of credit ("HELOC") as an option for an emergency fund (or at least to supplement an emergency fund)[48]. A HELOC allows you to borrow up to a certain amount of your home's equity (usually 80-85%). Because it's a line of credit, the thought is that it is "there when you need it," but you don't actually draw on the line of credit (i.e., borrow the money) until there is an emergency. <u>At first glance, I suppose this doesn't sound like a terrible idea. But let's think about it a little deeper. Why would I want to respond to a financial emergency by going deeper into debt?</u> This isn't free money. It's a variable interest rate loan that can change as often as once a month, and it is secured by a lien on your house. If you can't make the payments, you could lose your home! <u>Adding more debt can turn a financial emergency into a financial crisis. Your emergency fund should be in cold, hard cash!</u> If you feel like you need an extra layer of protection beyond your current emergency fund, don't get a HELOC (which will require you to pay interest) – save more cash and let it earn interest for you!

Previously, we discussed being both gazelle and cheetah intense while eliminating your debt in Step Two. In Step Three, your debt

---

[48] https://www.experian.com/blogs/ask-experian/can-i-use-heloc-as-emergency-fund/

is no longer chasing you. This necessarily causes the gazelle part of your intensity to fall away. <u>You will find that you won't want or need to run like your life depends upon it. That's okay! It doesn't. I want you to continue pursuing your financial goals like a cheetah, but it's fine to take the edge off a bit here</u>. Maybe you keep shopping the grocery store ads to keep that monthly food budget low, but you increase your restaurant budget from 10% of the grocery budget to 20%. Perhaps you take a legit (but still modest) vacation to celebrate becoming debt-free. We did both those things. But be careful! This is not an excuse to overspend or go back into debt. We upgraded from McDonald's to Outback Steakhouse (not Ruth's Chris), and we vacationed in Savannah/Hilton Head (not Tahiti) instead of at our nearest national park.

Step three is about protecting you and your family in an emergency. However, you also need to ensure you are covered in the event of the ultimate emergency – death. What would you and your family's finances look like if you and/or your spouse died? <u>This is where life insurance comes in</u>. Life insurance is there to replace income when someone dies. It can also help cover the costs of hiring a non-parent to care for children if the primary caregiving parent passes away.

There are two types of life insurance: 1) whole/permanent life (which is more of an investment option (and not a particularly good one) that we will cover in Chapter 10) and 2) term life. In a term life insurance policy, you will pay a monthly insurance premium in exchange for the promise that the insurance company will pay a fixed "death benefit" to the listed beneficiary (typically your spouse and/or children) if the person whose life is covered dies during the "term" of the policy. The term is usually ten or twenty years. The longer the term of the policy, the larger the death benefit, and the more likely the insurance company thinks it is that the covered person will die during the term (based on age or health issues), the more expensive the monthly premium will be.

Sometimes, the premium will increase over time. Always shop for "level-term" policies (where the premium remains the same for the life of the policy).

So, when do I need life insurance? If anyone in your life relies on you for their financial well-being, your life needs to be insured. Okay, how much do I need? Let's go through some scenarios:

- **Single with no debt.** You may want to think about a small policy to cover final expenses. If you have enough saved to cover those, don't worry about life insurance – yet.

- **Single with debt.** Get a policy that will pay off the debt and any funeral/burial costs.

- **Married with no kids.** In this case, we are really only concerned with replacing income. So, if a spouse doesn't work, there's no huge reason to obtain a policy on their life. For any spouse earning income, the rule of thumb is to buy a policy with a death benefit equal to 10-12 times that spouse's annual income. The thought is that this amount can be invested and spit out enough income each year to replace what the deceased spouse was making.

- **Married with young children.** Here, in addition to replacing income, we need to think about paying for child care. If both spouses work full-time, the calculus is the same as above. We simply need to replace the deceased spouse's income, and that will take care of paying for child care so the surviving spouse can work. However, if one spouse is the stay-at-home mom or dad, we need to estimate the annual childcare cost we are currently saving. You then purchase a policy with a death benefit equal to 10-12 times that amount. That should put you in a spot where you can invest the insurance payout and receive enough income from those investments to cover child care.

Stop Choosing

- **To hope an emergency won't happen to you.** Maybe it won't – but why not be prepared, just in case it does?

- **To count a HELOC or unused credit card as your emergency fund.** Throwing more debt at your emergency is like tossing gasoline on a fire. Someone is going to get hurt.

- **To keep your emergency fund in a checking or savings account that pays little or no interest.** Use a high-yield savings account instead (Ally, SoFi, Citizens Bank, and Capital One are good examples).

Start Choosing

- **To eliminate financial uncertainty from your life.** When you have a fully-funded emergency fund, you don't have to wonder, "What will I do if my car breaks down? Or I have to visit the emergency room? Or I lose my job?" Your emergency fund is there to cover all of that.

- **Better sleep.** Because it eliminates uncertainty, your emergency fund will reduce your anxiety. You will wake up in a cold sweat much less often than you did before!

- **To treat your emergency fund as insurance – not an investment.** Don't put it in anything that has the possibility of going down in value. No mutual funds, stocks, or crypto allowed!

7

STEP FOUR - INVEST (ABOUT) 15% OF YOUR HOUSEHOLD INCOME IN RETIREMENT

You will tackle Baby Steps 4-6 (saving for retirement, saving for your kids' college, and paying off your mortgage early) simultaneously. However, they are listed in order of importance. Why is saving for retirement more important than saving for college or paying off your home early? Let's start with saving for college for your kids. Kids can save for college themselves. They can work while in school. They can earn scholarships. They may not go to college at all (it's not for everyone). And, frankly, you don't have a moral obligation to pay for your kids' college, but you do have a moral obligation to be self-reliant – even when you can no longer work. Okay, why not attack the mortgage debt like we attacked all our other debt? Well, primarily, it's because your home will likely increase in value. You want to kill your mortgage as soon as possible – but not at the expense of funding your retirement.

It's also okay to want to have a fun and rewarding retirement! And – News Flash – spending your golden years living meagerly because your only source of income is Social Security or working at Walmart is neither fun nor rewarding!

Let's get the party started with some frightening retirement statistics:

- About one in four American adults, including one in eight adults age 60 or older, have no retirement savings [49].

- The median 401k balance for people 55-64 (you know, the folks closest to retirement) is just under $85,000[50].

- 46% of American adults have less than $15,000 saved for retirement[51].

- As of July 2023, the average monthly Social Security benefit check is $1,703.98[52]. For most of us, $20k a year just ain't gonna cut it – and even that amount assumes that Social Security will still be there when you retire. There are no guarantees it will[53].

- Despite all this bad news on the retirement front, only 17% of Americans identified "saving for retirement" as their top financial priority for 2022[54].

Let's talk about that last number for a minute. Why is this percentage so low? Well, "saving for retirement" came in third in that survey behind "increasing savings" (40%) and "paying off debt" (30%). This tells me that 70% of Americans are in Steps One through Three. In and of itself, this is not a problem. The problem

---

[49] https://www.pwc.com/us/en/industries/financial-services/library/retirement-in-america.html
[50] https://institutional.vanguard.com/content/dam/inst/vanguard-has/insights-pdfs/22_TL_HAS_FullReport_2022.pdf
[51] https://www.cnbc.com/2022/03/31/saving-for-retirement-is-top-financial-priority-for-just-17percent-of-adults.html
[52] https://www.ssa.gov/policy/docs/quickfacts/stat_snapshot/
[53] https://www.cnbc.com/select/will-social-security-run-out-heres-what-you-need-to-know/
[54] https://www.cnbc.com/2022/03/31/saving-for-retirement-is-top-financial-priority-for-just-17percent-of-adults.html

is that most of the 70% are stuck in a vicious cycle of debt where they will never finish Step Two or Three. They accumulate things (cars, clothes, vacations, furniture), often using debt, but they live without any financial plan or direction. They'd like to be out of debt, have more savings, and save for retirement, but they either don't know what to do or refuse to make the intentional financial decisions necessary to get there. So, I'm saying that if you've worked through the first three Steps and arrived at a place where saving for retirement is your top financial priority, take a moment (or maybe even a few moments) to celebrate! <u>You are way ahead of most Americans – regardless of your age!</u>

The first major question is, why 15%? Research has shown that starting early and saving 15% of your pre-tax income for retirement will almost always allow you to retire on time (around age 65) and do so comfortably. A 15% savings rate should also allow you the wiggle room you need to save for college (Step 5) and pay off your home early (Step 6) at the same time. Please be aware that the 15% retirement savings recommendation is not just a Ramsey thing – it is pretty standard across the financial industry. I found 15% as a rule of thumb from Fidelity[55], T. Rowe Price[56], Forbes[57], and others. Once you have completed Steps One through Three, I can't think of any good reason to save less than 15% for retirement, unless you are retired. Okay, so why would you save more than 15%? I can think of a few reasons:

1) **You started late.** Several experts suggest bumping the savings rate to 25-30% or more if you are beginning to save for retirement in your 40s or later. This makes sense, as you

---

[55] https://www.fidelity.com/viewpoints/retirement/how-much-money-should-I-save
[56] https://www.troweprice.com/content/dam/iinvestor/planning-and-research/t-rowe-price-insights/retirement-and-planning/pdfs/aiming-for-a-15--savings-goal.pdf
[57] https://www.forbes.com/sites/qai/2022/11/02/retirement-savings-by-age-max-out-your-potential/?sh=69fb76d42e2b

will have less time for the magic of compound interest to work in your favor.

2) **You want to retire early.** If you want to retire at 50 or 55, you will need to save more now than you would if you are content retiring at 65 or 67.

3) **You don't have any kids, or they have already attended college.** If you don't need to worry about helping to send your kids to college debt-free, then you can put more towards a sweet retirement.

4) **You've already paid off your mortgage.** Once you've kicked Fannie Mae to the curb, you can (and probably should) increase your retirement savings.

Okay, sweet, I need to save at least 15% of my pre-tax income for retirement – now what? Well, I like to think of saving for retirement as a road trip from wherever you are now to your ideal retirement destination (Florida? Arizona? Texas? Southern Utah?). To be as efficient as possible, you need to make two critical decisions:

1) What vehicle(s) are you going to take?
2) What road(s) do you want to travel?

The "vehicles" here are the different types of retirement accounts available. Primarily, we are talking about Individual Retirement Arrangements/Accounts ("IRAs") and employer-sponsored accounts (the most common of which is the 401k Plan, but there are also several others – like 403bs and 457s). IRAs and 401ks also come in Roth and Traditional flavors. Let's go through the most common retirement vehicles:

- **Traditional IRAs**
- **Roth IRAs**

- **Traditional 401ks**
- **Roth 401ks**

Let's compare each retirement "vehicle" to actual vehicles that you would take on the highway.

Traditional IRA → Mazda Miata

IRAs are tax-advantaged savings accounts the government has established to allow Americans to save for retirement. Traditional IRAs came into existence with the passage of the Employee Retirement Income Security Act of 1974 (ERISA). The tax advantages of a Traditional IRA are:

- As long as you are not covered by an employer-sponsored retirement plan at work (or you are, but you make less than $73,000 single or $116,000 married filing jointly), the entire amount of your Traditional IRA contribution is tax deductible in the year you make the contribution[58].

- There is no tax on any gains or income derived from Traditional IRA investments at the time of the gain or income. For example, if you bought Amazon stock in your Traditional IRA in 1997 and sold it now, you would pay no taxes on the rather sizable gain resulting from that transaction.

So, I get a tax deduction for my contributions and don't pay taxes on any gains/income from the Traditional IRA's investments? That sounds awesome! What's the catch? Good observation – there's always a catch with the IRS! The catch is that all withdrawals from a Traditional IRA are taxed at ordinary income tax rates, and (with some narrow exceptions) all

---

[58] https://www.irs.gov/newsroom/401k-limit-increases-to-22500-for-2023-ira-limit-rises-to-6500

withdrawals before age 59 ½ are subject to a 10% early withdrawal penalty. Also, the IRS doesn't allow Traditional IRA investments to roll tax-free forever. They want their taxes before you die (if they can get them). As such, they require Traditional IRA owners to start taking Required Minimum Distributions (RMDs) at age 72-75 (depending on the year when you will reach the applicable age). The RMD amounts are taxable.

The maximum contribution to a Traditional IRA in 2023 is $6,500 (for those under age 50) and $7,500 (for those 50 and older)[59]. You (or your spouse) must have earned income of at least the amount of your IRA contribution. The contribution limits periodically increase to keep pace with inflation. The contribution limit was $1,500 from 1974-81.

So, why is a Traditional IRA like a Mazda Miata? Three reasons:

1) **It doesn't have much room.** As we will discuss later, employer-sponsored retirement vehicles have (potentially much) higher contribution limits. You can get more into them.

2) **It's fast and sexy.** The tax deduction you get right now for making contributions is undoubtedly desirable, and it can free up the cash you need to make the maximum contribution each year.

3) **It may not look or run as great in 30 years.** All Traditional IRA distributions are subject to ordinary income taxes, and eventually (age 72-75), the government will require you to start taking distributions so they can tax you. This means the 65-year-old version of you will probably wish you had picked a different retirement vehicle – just like that same

---

[59] https://www.irs.gov/newsroom/401k-limit-increases-to-22500-for-2023-ira-limit-rises-to-6500

version of you may wish you had never bought that Miata.

Roth IRA – Toyota Prius

Let's start with what Roth and Traditional IRAs have in common:

1) **Contribution Limits.** They are the same as Traditional IRAs - $6,500 (for those under age 50) and $7,500 (for those 50 and older). You (or your spouse) must have earned income of at least the amount of your IRA contribution.

2) **No Tax on Gains/Income.** There is no tax on any gains or income derived from Roth IRA investments at the time of the gain or income. So, if you bought Bitcoin in your Roth IRA for $500 per coin and sold it in 2021 for $50,000/ per coin, you would pay no taxes on that gain.

What are the differences? The main one is that the tax treatment on contributions and distributions is reversed from Traditional IRAs. The Roth IRA owner gets no deduction for making contributions – so there is no tax break for you right now. However, as long as you wait to take distributions until after age 59 ½, all such distributions are tax-free. So, while gains in a Traditional IRA are tax-*deferred*, gains in a Roth IRA are tax-*free*. You can also always withdraw up to the amount of your Roth IRA contributions tax and penalty-free (even before age 59 ½).

One major quirk of Roth IRAs is that there are income restrictions on making direct Roth contributions. In 2023, you cannot contribute to a Roth IRA if you make more than $138,000 (Single) or $218,000 (Married Filing Jointly). However, since 2010, there have been no income restrictions on the ability to *convert* funds to Roth. This is where the "Backdoor Roth IRA" strategy comes into play. Here are the steps to the "Backdoor" strategy:

Step 1: Fund a New Non-Deductible Traditional IRA. This IRA is "non-deductible" because high-income earners who participate in a company retirement plan (or who have a spouse who does) are also restricted from making "deductible" contributions to a Traditional IRA. However, such an account can be funded by non-deductible amounts up to the IRA annual contribution limit of $6,500 or $7,500. Because this contribution is "non-deductible," you don't get a tax deduction for it. However, you don't want or need that deduction because you plan to convert that contribution to Roth anyway. In fact, if you did get a deduction for the contribution, you'd have to pay taxes on the amounts later converted to Roth.

Step 2: Convert the Non-Deductible Traditional IRA Funds to Roth. You will contact your IRA custodian and tell them you wish to convert the amounts contributed to Roth.

Okay, so why is a Roth IRA like a Toyota Prius?

- **It won't hold much.** Let's just say that our Prius wasn't a lot of help the last time we moved. The contribution limits are the same for Roth IRAs as Traditional IRAs (and the limits are relatively low).

- **It ain't sexy right now.** Nobody ever impressed a date by rolling up in a Prius. I was already married when I bought mine, but no one has ever checked me out at a stoplight while I've been driving it (maybe that says more about me than the Prius). Anyway, Roth IRAs provide no relief on your current-year tax bill when you make a contribution. There's no deduction.

- **It's efficient and reliable.** The Prius sips gas, has almost no maintenance costs, and just runs and runs. I plan to bestow mine upon my oldest daughter when she gets her driver's license in a couple years. When you're in retirement, you'll be glad you chose it. Those tax-free distributions after 59 ½ are pretty sweet – just like a paid-for Prius that keeps running and costs almost nothing to insure or maintain.

Traditional 401k – GMC Yukon XL Denali

Unlike IRAs, 401k's are employer-sponsored tax-advantaged retirement plans. Many employers establish these plans to attract and retain employees. The tax advantages of a Traditional 401k are the same as a Traditional IRA. Your contributions are tax-deductible, and your investments within the account will grow tax-deferred. When you withdraw funds from the account, you will pay taxes (and possibly early withdrawal penalties).

There are two main differences between a Traditional 401k and a Traditional IRA:

1) **The contribution limits are much higher.** Employees can contribute up to 100% of their W-2 compensation from the business, with a cap of $22,500, for 2023. Employees age 50 or older can make a "catch-up" contribution of an additional $7,500 – for a total contribution limit of $30,000[60].

2) **In most cases, the employer must match a portion of the employee's contribution.** This is a nice perk of the 401k for rank-and-file employees, as the employer match is essentially "free money" for the employee.

The total contribution limit (adding together employee and employer contributions) for 2023 is $66,000 for employees under age 50. Because of the $7,500 catch-up contribution, the overall

---

[60] https://www.irs.gov/newsroom/401k-limit-increases-to-22500-for-2023-ira-limit-rises-to-6500

limit is $73,500 for folks 50 and older[61].

The vast majority of employees will never flirt with these overall contribution limits. This is primarily because 401k plans are not permitted to discriminate in favor of the owners or highly compensated employees by giving them larger employer contributions than the rank-and-file. As such, employer contributions are typically quite limited.

I think an example will help to demonstrate what I mean. Let's use the terms of KKOS Lawyers' (my employer) 401k plan, which are very common. In our plan, the firm will match 100% of all employee contributions up to 3% of the employee's salary and 50% from 3-5% of the employee's salary. Let's say a KKOS employee (age 40) has a salary of $250,000 and contributes the maximum ($22,500) to the 401k. KKOS will provide a 100% match for the first $7,500 contributed by the employee (an additional $7,500) because $7,500 is 3% of the employee's salary. KKOS will provide a 50% match for the next $5,000 contributed by the employee (an additional $2,500) because $5,000 is another 2% of the employee's salary. So, even on a healthy $250,000 salary, the maximum that could be contributed to a Traditional 401k for a KKOS employee under age 50 is $32,500 ($22,500 employee contribution + $10,000 employer contribution). That isn't even half of the $66,000 limit!

Well, what if I am self-employed and have no full-time employees? In that case, the IRS isn't worried about the 401k plan discriminating against rank-and-file employees in favor of the owners – because there are no rank-and-file employees. Small business owners in this situation can establish what the IRS calls a One-Participant 401k Plan[62]. The One-Participant 401k is commonly known as a Solo 401k. The Solo 401k allows small

---

[61] https://directedira.com/irs-2023-contribution-limits/
[62] https://www.irs.gov/retirement-plans/one-participant-401k-plans

business owners to supercharge their retirement savings.

Let me give you an example. Let's take a 40-year-old real estate agent with no employees whose business (which is (as it should be) an S-Corporation) pays them an annual salary of $150,000. That business establishes a Solo 401k Plan. The employee contribution limit is still 100% of the W-2 salary with a cap of $22,500 – that part does not change. The major change is in the employer contribution. Because we don't have to worry about discriminating against other employees, the employer contribution limit is 25% of the W-2 salary. 25% of $150,000 is $37,500. So, while a KKOS Lawyers employee with a $250,000 salary can only get $32,500 into the company Traditional 401k, an entrepreneur with no employees can get $60,000 into their Solo Traditional 401k on a $150,000 salary. Additionally, the entire $60,000 would be a tax deduction for the entrepreneur, while the KKOS employee only gets a deduction for their employee contribution ($22,500).

Now, let's take a step back. Just because the tax code allows you (as a business owner) to make such a large Solo 401k contribution doesn't mean you will necessarily have the cash available to do so. Further, even if the money is available, if such a large contribution would exceed 15% of your income, consideration should be given to whether the excess would be better deployed by saving for kids' college or paying down your mortgage (Steps Five and Six).

What makes the Traditional 401k like a GMC Yukon XL Denali?

1) **There's a ton of room.** The high contribution limits mean you can get a lot of stuff (cash) in there.

2) **It looks fantastic right now.** The Yukon Denali is a stunner. It will turn heads. Similarly, the colossal deduction will sparkle on your current-year tax return.

3) **It depreciates quickly and guzzles gas.** Just like with the Traditional IRA, all distributions are subject to ordinary income taxes, and eventually (age 72-75), the government will require you to start taking distributions so they can tax you. So, just like with the Denali, eventually, the Traditional 401k isn't worth quite as much as you thought.

Roth 401k – Ford Bronco Hybrid

A Roth 401k is an employer-sponsored retirement plan that allows the employee to make after-tax contributions that will grow tax-free instead of pre-tax contributions that will grow tax-deferred (which is the case in a Traditional 401k). <u>The contribution limits are the same as in a Traditional 401k, and unlike a Roth IRA – there is no income limit!</u> Also, (and this is new with the passage of the Secure Act 2.0 in late 2022) required minimum distributions are not required in Roth 401ks starting in 2024[63].

If you want to participate in a Roth 401k, you need to know a few things:

1) Not all 401k plans provide a Roth option.

2) Even in plans that provide a Roth option, the first-line people you speak with at your 401k administrator may not be aware of it. Keep pressing.

3) Before the passage of the SECURE Act 2.0 in late 2022, the employer contributions in a 401k plan had to be Traditional, pre-tax funds. The law now allows plans to permit employees to ask that employer contributions be Roth funds. However, please be aware that it will take quite some time – possibly years – for 401k plan language to be

---

[63] https://www.usbank.com/retirement-planning/financial-perspectives/saving-for-retirement-secure-act.html

amended to allow for this. Even then, it is not something plans are required to permit. Also, don't forget that if you choose for the employer contributions to be Roth, you will be taxed on the amount of those contributions. Your plan may also allow you to convert the Traditional employer contributions to Roth.

Ok, why is the Roth 401k like a Ford Bronco Hybrid?

1) **It's roomy.** Maybe not as roomy as the Yukon XL Denali (Traditional 401k) because the employer contributions will likely be Traditional (and you may not be able to convert them to Roth), but you can fit a lot more contributions into the Roth 401k than the Roth IRA.

2) **It's sexy - but not as sexy as a Yukon Denali.** You are giving up a significant tax deduction now. So (at least temporarily), you might feel like you're missing out.

3) **You'll probably be happy about it in the long run.** Of the options we've discussed, this one allows you to get the largest amount into a vehicle that will grow tax-free. It is what I do. I make Roth 401k employee contributions and allow the employer contributions to remain Traditional.

You're probably saying, "Thanks for the fun analogies, Jarom, but what vehicle makes the most sense for me?" Well, first of all, you don't necessarily have to choose one. You can use multiple vehicles at the same time. I also (usually) prefer Roth (paying taxes now) to Traditional (paying taxes later). This is for two reasons:

1) **I am eternally optimistic about how my investments will perform.** As such, I would rather pay taxes now on my contributions than pay taxes later on the (massive, of course) growth of the investments I make with those funds.

2) **I am eternally pessimistic about what the government will do regarding anything (especially taxes).** I think it's pretty certain that tax rates will generally be higher in the future than they are now. Because of this, I would rather pay my taxes now.

The better you think your investments will do, the more time you have to let them grow before you need the money, and the higher you think tax rates will be in the future, the more sense it makes to go with Roth over Traditional.

Here is my hierarchy:

1) **Get your employer match (if you have one) first.** If you work for someone else and they have a 401k plan where they match some or all of your contributions, then go get that free money! Don't move on to another vehicle until you have gotten all of it. If your employer allows your employee contributions to be Roth dollars, I would take advantage of that option.

2) **If you have a side hustle or small business without any non-family employees, consider establishing a Solo 401k Plan and maxing out your remaining Roth 401k employee contributions there.** The main reason to go here next is that your investment options open up in a Solo 401k. You can set up the Solo 401k at a brokerage where you will have more options than you would with most employer plans. We also help people who want to self-direct their Solo 401ks into investments outside the stock market (like real estate, cryptocurrency, and early-stage private offerings). We will discuss self-directing in greater detail below.

3) **If your employer 401k does not allow Roth employee contributions, max out contributions to a Roth IRA.**

You can make Roth IRA contributions even if you are covered by a plan at work and even if your income exceeds the Roth IRA contribution limits (using the Backdoor Roth IRA method described above). However, if you have existing Traditional IRA accounts, please be aware that to avoid potential adverse tax consequences, you would need to convert the existing Traditional IRAs to Roth before pursuing the Backdoor Roth IRA method. If you are married, max out Roth IRA contributions for both spouses.

4) **If your employer 401k allows Roth employee contributions (and you like the investment options in the employer plan), you can choose to max out your Roth 401k contributions before moving on to the Roth IRA(s).** Many employer 401k plans have limited investment options, so if you want to invest in different market products or self-direct your investments, you will need to move on to the Roth IRA(s), max out those contributions, and then come back to the Roth 401k. If you are good with your employer plan investment options, you can max out the employee Roth contributions in that plan before moving out to Roth IRAs.

5) **If you want to make additional Roth contributions after reaching the employee contribution limits, speak with a tax professional about the possibility of a "Mega Backdoor Roth[64]."**

6) **If you have exhausted your Roth options and still have the ability to do so, max out your Traditional 401k employee contributions in your employer 401k.**

In a nutshell: Match > Roth > Traditional – and if you can get a match on Roth contributions in an employer-sponsored 401k,

---

[64] https://www.nerdwallet.com/article/investing/mega-backdoor-roths-work

make sure you do that. It's what I do!

Ok. You've decided on your retirement destination. You've selected your vehicle(s). <u>The last decision is what roads you will take to get there</u>. In this context, the "roads" are the investments you will make. I have divided your choices into three primary groups:

1) **The Interstate (Stock Market Investments).** These are the most traveled roads. Most retirement investments are in publicly traded stocks, bonds, mutual funds, exchange-traded funds, etc. Why? Just like the interstate, they're easy. Set the cruise control and forget it. There's not a lot of maintenance. Jump on the freeway and get off at your retirement exit. However, the interstate doesn't always go exactly where you need it to go. It can be boring and prone to traffic jams. Sometimes there is a faster and more rewarding way to get where you're going if you are willing to be a bit more adventurous. This is where the second type of road comes in.

2) **The Backroad Shortcuts (Self-Directed Investments).** What do I mean when I say "self-directed investments?" I don't mean a plan where you select your own brokerage products. <u>I mean investments outside the stock market – real estate, cryptocurrency, pre-IPO businesses, Super Bowl tickets, head of cattle, etc. Wait, I can use 401k or IRA money to invest in stuff like that? Yes – you can!</u> What you can't do is make investments like this in your account at Fidelity or Schwab. They won't allow it because they make substantially less money when you don't use their brokerage products to invest. You are permitted to use retirement dollars to invest in anything other than:

- Collectibles such as art, stamps, certain coins, alcoholic beverages, or antiques[65]
- Life insurance[66]
- S-Corporation stock[67]

You may not know what makes for a great mutual fund, but maybe you know a great real estate deal when you see one. Perhaps you know which cryptocurrency will be the next Bitcoin. Maybe you know of a startup or two that will make it big. You can make all of these investments with a self-directed retirement account – and the tax treatment on the appreciation (not to mention any rent or interest income) is exactly the same as on a publicly traded stock or mutual fund. <u>To make this happen, you will need an account with a self-directed retirement account custodian</u>. A self-directed custodian is simply one that will allow you to make all legal investments with your account. At KKOS Lawyers, we refer folks interested in self-directing their retirement to Directed IRA (directedira.com). This is for two reasons: 1) They do great work and are highly rated by their customers. 2) The company was founded by our partners here at KKOS (Mat Sorensen (whose *Self-Directed IRA Handbook* is the Bible of the self-directed IRA industry) and Mark Kohler).

<u>Just like when you decide to get off the Interstate and take a shortcut through the backroads, you'd better be prepared to be hands-on when you self-direct</u>. You are largely responsible for your own due diligence. It is much easier to commit what the IRS calls a "prohibited transaction[68]" (such as buying a vacation rental with your retirement account dollars and deciding to stay in it while on a trip with your

---

[65] IRC § 408(m)
[66] IRC § 408(a)(3)
[67] IRC § 1361(b)(1)(B)
[68] IRC § 4975

family). If you're not paying attention, you can run into unexpected taxes, such as Unrelated Business Income Tax (UBIT) and Unrelated Debt Financed Income (UDFI) tax. Because of these issues, it can help to stop and ask for directions to make sure you avoid these problems. This is where a good tax attorney (like me or one of my colleagues at KKOS Lawyers) can help you avoid making any wrong turns.

Also, just like how a shortcut sometimes turns out not to be a shortcut, self-directed investments do not bat a thousand. But when they work, they can offer returns well above what you can typically get in the market. There are no guarantees, but the self-directed backroad shortcut may help you supercharge your savings and deliver you to your retirement destination much faster than the stock market Interstate.

3) **Some Interstate and Some Backroads.** You don't have to choose 100% of one or the other. There is nothing wrong with doing both! Financial advisors call it "diversification," and it's a good thing! Sometimes, it makes sense to stay on the freeway, and sometimes you're so glad you got off and bypassed all the traffic by taking the backroads. Having some retirement in the market and some in alternative investments seems like the best of both worlds.

Okay, while we're on the topic of retirement, what about Social Security? When should I start taking those benefits? There are thousands of articles on the subject (almost 33,000 as of September 2023). For those born in 1960 or later, the full Social Security retirement age is 67. However, you can start taking Social Security benefits as early as age 62. The problem is that the government reduces your benefits when you start early. If you start at 62, your monthly benefit is only 70% of what it would be if you had waited until age 67. As you wait, that percentage increases. It looks like this:

Age 62 – 70%
Age 63 – 75%
Age 64 – 80%
Age 65 – 86.67%
Age 66 – 93.33%
Age 67 – 100%

The government also incentivizes waiting even longer to start taking benefits. The longer you wait (up until age 70), the larger your monthly benefit will be. It follows this scale:

Age 68 – 108%
Age 69 – 116%
Age 70 – 124%

Because of the increased benefit, the rule of thumb is that you should wait as long as possible (up to age 70) to start taking Social Security benefits – and I think that is excellent advice. Here's the thing, though. If you are <u>paying freaking attention and making intentional financial decisions</u> throughout your life, your Social Security benefits will be a small portion of your income in retirement. So, if you're doing it right, it won't really matter when you decide to take Social Security. If you act now, you can take the drama and stress out of your Social Security decision – because you'll be just fine even if Social Security really does dry up before you can start taking it.

Stop Choosing

- **To believe you'll never actually get that old.** Ignoring it won't change the fact that you are getting older. And every time you forget, you tear your calf muscle while skipping at work – believe me, I know from experience.

- **To rely on the government (or anyone else) to bail you out.** Social Security may be there when you want to retire – or it might not. Do you really want to take that chance? Fund your own retirement and use the extra Social Security income to spoil your grandkids!

- **A retirement where you can't get by without a job.** I'm all for working during retirement – if you want to, not because you have to.

- **To let Wall Street dictate your retirement investments.** Self-directing allows you to invest in what you know and take control of your retirement.

Start Choosing

- **Your own retirement adventure.** When you fail to plan and invest, your need to work to earn income will choose your "retirement" path for you.

- **Free money from your employer.** If your employer offers a match on your retirement account contributions, take advantage of it (regardless of age)! Don't leave that free money on the table!

- **Roth over Traditional.** Choose tax-free income and distributions in retirement over a (relatively small) tax deduction now.

- **Not to stress about when to take Social Security.** Because any benefit you may get is unimportant to your overall retirement picture.

8

STEP FIVE – SAVE FOR YOUR CHILDREN'S COLLEGE FUND

Let's start with what I think is an exceptionally uncontroversial statement: <u>education is important</u>. Benjamin Franklin is credited with saying, "An investment in knowledge pays the best interest." And while the value of an education is not solely measured in dollars and cents, the numbers back Mr. Franklin up. See the chart below from the federal Bureau of Labor Statistics[69]:

Educational attainment	Median usual weekly earnings ($)	Unemployment rate (%)
Doctoral Degree	1,909	1.5
Professional Degree	1,924	1.8
Master's Degree	1,574	2.6
Bachelor's Degree	1,334	3.5
Associate's Degree	963	4.6
Some college, no degree	899	5.5
High School Diploma	809	6.2
Less than a high school diploma	626	8.3
Total	1,057	4.7

---

[69] https://www.bls.gov/emp/tables/unemployment-earnings-education.htm

Note: Data are for persons age 25 and over. Earnings are for full-time wage and salary workers.
Source: Current Population Survey, U.S. Department of Labor, U.S. Bureau of Labor Statistics

The numbers don't lie. High school graduates make 30% more than high school dropouts, four-year college graduates earn 65% more than folks with a diploma only, and nabbing that doctorate or professional degree will net you about 44% more than settling for a bachelor's. Education makes you much less likely to be unemployed as well. Dropouts are more than twice as likely to be looking for work than those with a bachelor's degree, and those who never went to college are about four times more likely to be out of work than people with doctorates or professional degrees.

I think we all agree that education is important, and the numbers verify that it dramatically increases one's earning capacity – so what is there to argue about? Plenty, as it turns out. Here are a few controversial topics when it comes to education:

- Should everyone go to college?
- Do parents have a moral obligation to help their children pay for college?
- If they decide to help, how much of a child's education expenses should parents pay?
- Are student loans a net good for society?
- How much in student loans is it "ok" to borrow?
- Should the government be involved in the student loan business at all?
- Should the government forgive anyone's student loans? If so, whose?

Let's tackle a few of these questions.

Do Parents Have a Moral Obligation to Help Their Children Pay for College?

I think "obligation" is a strong word in this context. I don't think any parent has an obligation to pay anything towards a child's college education – let alone cover college 100%. However, I think parents do have an obligation to change the current paradigm and mindset that says, "Student loans are the only way to go to college" and "whatever college costs is worth it." Neither of those statements is true – and the belief that they are is the reason for our nation's current $1.77 trillion student loan crisis.

With that being said, as a father of three (one of whom just started high school), I feel a great desire to help my kids pay for college if they choose to go. Because of my experience with student debt, I am especially anxious to help my kids get through school without resorting to student loans. Other parents would argue that children must learn to take care of themselves and handle their lives responsibly, so they believe it is counterproductive for a parent to step in and pay for a college education. I can certainly see the wisdom in this school of thought. But I think there is a balance to be struck – which leads to the next question.

If You Decide to Help, How Much of a Child's Education Expenses Should You Pay?

This is a profoundly personal and circumstance-dependent question, so there is no single "correct" answer. With that in mind, here are my thoughts:

- **Don't feel guilty if you are unable to help.** Most importantly, don't compound the problem by borrowing money yourself to help. Jeopardizing your financial situation in this way will only make things worse.

- **Don't feel like you need to pay for everything.** I love the idea of the child having some "skin in the game." There's nothing wrong with requiring a young adult to work to pay for room and board, books, transportation, spending money, etc. In fact, I think it's a healthy way to help instill a good work ethic in our children.

- **Don't be afraid to set boundaries.** My wife and I have agreed to pay for undergraduate tuition and books for our kids at a public in-state college or Brigham Young University (which is cheaper than in-state tuition at the University of Utah (where we live) for members of the Church of Jesus Christ of Latter-day Saints). According to an October 2021 study by the College Board, the average annual in-state public school tuition is $10,740. The average yearly out-of-state tuition is $27,560. Going out of state may be a fantastic "experience," but a degree from the University of (your home state) will end up being just as valuable as a degree from the University of (some other state). My wife and I have decided we won't subsidize an additional $17,000/year for an "experience." The same goes for a degree from that pricey private university (with the possible exception of an Ivy League school or Stanford). I love my kids (and they're pretty smart), but I don't know if they are Ivy League material. I guess we'll cross that bridge if we ever get there. Your boundaries don't have to be the same as ours, but setting some will be healthy for you and your children.

- **Don't raid your emergency fund or retirement accounts to pay for college.** During the airline pre-flight safety briefing, the flight attendant always instructs passengers to secure their oxygen masks before placing masks on any children traveling with them in the event of a change in cabin pressure. The same principle applies here. These steps are presented in order of importance. Saving for your children's college education is Step Five. Do not undo your completion of Step Two or Three or sacrifice your progress on Step Four to work on Step Five. Do not worry about saving for college until and unless you are out of debt, have a fully-funded emergency fund, and are saving approximately 15% of your income for retirement.

- **Don't co-sign on your kids' student loans.** I don't see student loans as a blessing, so I don't think it makes sense to help facilitate my kids being able to incur that debt. I also don't want to be on the hook if my kids fail to repay their loans (and if they turn out to be punks like their dad). More than the financial burden, I don't want to subject my relationship with them to that additional stress.

How Much in Student Loans Is It "Okay" to Borrow?

For 99% or more of undergraduate degrees, my answer is simple – <u>nothing.</u> Getting a Bachelor's degree debt-free will require some combination of the following three things:

1) **Planning and saving.** Having a head start always helps, and having a chunk of change set aside and ready to go when it's time to start spending gives you that head start. The longer you save for education, the more the magic of compound interest can work in your favor. With that being said, it's never too late. There's also no shame in putting school on hold in favor of working for a year or two to get that education nest egg in place. Planning includes scouring the planet and the internet for potential grants and scholarships. The following websites are good places to start (and come back to during) your scholarship journey:

    - **Scholarships.com** (https://www.scholarships.com/)
    - **College Board/Big Future** (https://bigfuture.collegeboard.org/pay-for-college/scholarship-search)

- **Fastweb** (https://www.fastweb.com/)
- **Scholarship Owl** (https://scholarshipowl.com/)
- **Going Merry** (https://www.goingmerry.com/)
- **Cappex** (https://www.cappex.com/)
- **Bold.org** (https://bold.org/)
- **Scholly** (https://myscholly.com/)
- **CareerOneStop/U.S. Department of Labor** (https://www.careeronestop.org/toolkit/training/find-scholarships.aspx?curPage=1&awardTypefilter=Scholarship)

Another tip - planning and saving work best when the student and the parents work on these goals together. Without support from mom and dad, most kids won't know where to start and will give up almost immediately if they do start – but parents won't drag the dead weight of an unmotivated and uncooperative student very far, either.

2) **Work.** It is almost impossible to get through an undergraduate degree debt-free without some sort of employment. Depending on the situation, it may be part-time or full-time work.

3) **Patience and sacrifice.** Your child (or maybe you) may need to sacrifice the experience of going to that "dream school." There will also be sacrifices when it comes to housing, vacations, cars, and time.

As you know, I didn't work or sacrifice much during my college years. I took out student loans and started racking up credit card debt. However, one of my roommates (who is still one of my best friends) took a different path. He went to school full-time but also had a job stocking shelves almost every day at one of the local grocery stores. He would come home most nights around 9-10 p.m. – right when the rest of us in the apartment were just getting ramped up for an evening of video games or other mindless entertainment. He would grab something to eat and either just crash on the couch or go up to his room to sleep. If we were going out, he almost always stayed home. I honestly always wondered why he was so freaking tired. It turns out that's what happens when you go to school full-time and hold down a full-time job. <u>However, his sacrifice paid significant dividends</u>. He graduated from BYU with no credit card debt and no student loans. He was on the path to financial freedom immediately. He didn't need a quasi-religious experience at age 41 to get there.

<u>When it comes to graduate school, my rule of thumb is that you should not incur more debt than the median annual first-year salary for graduates of the school you attend</u>. If you pursue a graduate-level degree, I want you to do the opposite of what I did in law school. Don't use credit cards to support your lifestyle, and do everything you can to avoid taking on any student loan debt whatsoever. Think about taking a year (or two) to work, live cheaply (maybe even at home), and save money toward the cost of your graduate studies. Make affordability (both tuition and the cost of living in the city where the school is located) a priority when deciding where to study. <u>Do not "wander" into graduate school because you don't know what else to do next</u>. Your decision to go to graduate school must be intentional. It is crucial that you understand how and why (and frankly, if) your chosen graduate degree will increase your earning capacity before you commit. In short, the same principles of planning and saving, work, and patience and sacrifice will still apply when it comes to graduate school.

However, I understand that graduate school is different. It's more expensive than a bachelor's degree. Many folks are married and/or starting a family during graduate school. It's much more of a long-term investment than an undergraduate degree. As such, the student loan calculus for graduate school is necessarily a bit different. <u>Do not incur more graduate school debt than the median first-year salary of graduates with your degree from the school you are looking to attend</u>. Every school you apply to should have this information. If they act like they don't want to give it to you – that is a very bad sign.

Based on the most recent statistics available (for the Class of 2021), this means someone attending law school at the same university I did (the University of Denver) should not incur more than $75,000 in debt to obtain their law degree there[70]. Harvard law school graduates, on the other hand, would be justified in incurring up to $201,250 in debt for their degrees[71]. <u>While there are no guarantees, following the "first-year salary" rule of thumb will help you ensure a sufficient return on your graduate school education investment</u>.

Here's one last bit of advice for those planning to go to school to be a doctor, dentist, lawyer, etc. (or already in school). Most of you will graduate with student loan debt. If you do, I implore you to keep your head down and concentrate on the long term. You may start with an income well into six figures. <u>However, if you have a half million dollars or more in student loan debt, you are a broke doctor, dentist, or lawyer</u>. Live that way for the first few months or years until you have cleared all your debts. You will then be left with decades to save, invest, and yes – even spend, free from the stress of debt hanging over your head.

Okay, you want to help our kids (or grandkids) go to college debt-free. What tools are available to help? <u>There are two primary tax-advantaged ways to save for college – they are 529 Plans and Coverdell Education Savings Accounts ("Coverdells")</u>. 529s and Coverdells have many similarities but also several important

---

[70] https://www.law.du.edu/careers/employment-statistics
[71] https://hls.harvard.edu/career-planning/recent-employment-data/

differences. The good news is that you don't have to choose one or the other. Let's review the similarities between these accounts.

<u>529 and Coverdell Similarities</u>

- **Both are funded with post-tax money (at least at the federal level).** There is currently no federal tax deduction for contributions to either 529s or Coverdells. However, over 30 states offer a limited state income tax deduction for 529 Plan contributions[72].

- **The growth in both is tax-free (as long as withdrawals are made for qualifying educational expenses).** So, both plans act like Roth IRAs – no deduction for contributions, but the growth is tax-free. Qualifying expenses include tuition and fees (including those for elementary, middle, and high schools, and any college, university, vocational school, or other postsecondary educational institution eligible to participate in a student aid program administered by the US Department of Education), required textbooks, room and board (subject to certain restrictions), computers and related equipment, and repayment of student loans.

- **Both can be transferred to another member of the beneficiary's family.** Suppose a beneficiary chooses not to go to college (or doesn't use all the funds in the account). In that case, the accounts can easily be switched to a member of the beneficiary's immediate or extended family (not the account owner's family).

- **Non-qualified distributions from both are subject to income tax and a 10% penalty on the earnings.** For example, let's say you've made $10,000 in contributions to

---

[72] https://www.savingforcollege.com/article/how-much-is-your-state-s-529-plan-tax-deduction-really-worth

either a 529 or a Coverdell. The investments you selected are now worth $15,000. If you want to pull out all $15,000 for a non-qualified purpose (perhaps to take a vacation), the $5,000 gain will be taxed at your marginal ordinary income tax rate. Let's assume yours is 22%. That means you will pay $1,100 in federal income tax on the withdrawal. You will also pay a $500 penalty (10% of the $5,000 gain).

529 and Coverdell Differences

- **Contribution Limits.** In the 529 Plan, there are technically no contribution limits. However, any contributions in a particular year from a single individual for a beneficiary exceeding the annual gift tax exemption amount ($17,000 for 2023) would necessitate the donor to file a federal Gift Tax return. 529 Plans also allow for a "Five-Year Election." Such an election would allow you to make five years of maximum contributions this year ($17,000 x 5 – for a total of $85,000) and spread out the contribution over five years for gift tax purposes. The contribution limit is the biggest drawback of the Coverdell. The limit is $2,000 per beneficiary (not per account established for that beneficiary). So, even if mom, dad, both sets of grandparents, and multiple aunts and uncles were willing to contribute money to a Coverdell for a particular beneficiary, the aggregate contributions for that beneficiary (regardless of the number of accounts involved) could not exceed $2,000 per year.

- **Income Restrictions on Contributions.** Your income will not affect your ability to make contributions to a 529 Plan. For Coverdells, the ability to contribute starts to phase out for individual filers making more than $95,000 and joint filers with incomes over $190,000. The ability to contribute to a Coverdell disappears entirely at $110,000 for individuals and $220,000 for joint filers. However, a "Back Door" method exists for high-income earners to open a Coverdell for their kids and get contributions into the account. Mom and/or Dad can open the Coverdell account and control it as the "Responsible Individual," but the Depositor can be someone else. This allows Mom and/or Dad to gift money to a friend or family member (under applicable gifting rules and limits) whose income would enable them to make a Coverdell contribution. The recipient of the gift makes the deposit into the Coverdell on behalf of the Beneficiary.

- **Beneficiary Age Restrictions.** There are none in a 529 Plan. 529 contributions can be made for a beneficiary of any age, and 529 funds can be used for qualifying education expenses of a beneficiary at any age. So, if I decide to set a goal to go back to school when I turn 50 (in five years), I could start a 529 account now and start throwing money in there. All principal and growth in the 529 would be tax-free for my qualifying educational expenses. With a Coverdell, on the other hand, no new contributions can be made once the account beneficiary reaches age 18 – and all account funds must be used by the time the beneficiary turns 30 (or the funds can be transferred to a different beneficiary).

- **Investment Options.** To this point, all the differences seem to weigh on the side of choosing a 529 over a Coverdell. 529s have no real contribution limits, income restrictions on contributions, or beneficiary age restrictions. Coverdells have all of those things. Many would cynically (but probably correctly) argue that the reason for all the 529 advantages is because of the one primary 529 disadvantage – the lack of investment options. Each state has its own 529 Plan program, but each only permits investments in some mix of (usually very conservative) mutual funds and FDIC-insured interest-bearing accounts. <u>In other words, 529 plans require "Wall Street" investments. Coverdells, on the other hand, can be self-directed into alternative assets like real estate, cryptocurrency, promissory notes, etc.</u> For many, the potential returns in alternative assets make Coverdells more attractive than 529s – despite the other disadvantages. The Wall Street lobby has worked very hard to keep self-directing out of Coverdells and ensure that 529s keep their advantages over Coverdells. They say it is to help keep investor funds "safe." Some would argue that it is really to keep their fees (which are often difficult to understand or even find) safe. However, if you want to make investments outside the stock market, an intelligent approach would be to max out Coverdell contributions first. You can then make 529 contributions with any additional funds you have earmarked for education savings.

Roth IRA for Education Savings

Another intriguing education savings option is the Roth IRA. <u>I want to be clear – I am not talking about a parent raiding their Roth IRA to pay for a child's education</u>. I do not favor that (remember, always heed the flight attendant's instruction to put on your mask first – then help your children with theirs). However, if a child has earned income, they can have <u>their own</u> Roth IRA. That earned income can come from their part-time job at the Gap. However, it can also come from their part-time job helping mom and dad market their business on social media or mowing lawns and doing touch-up painting on mom and dad's rental property.

Let the power of this strategy sink in for a minute - when your kids work for you, you can pay them a reasonable amount for their work (maybe $15-$20/hour, depending on their age, the task, and the amount of expertise they have). What you pay them is a legitimate business expense, meaning you won't pay taxes on that amount. All Americans have a Standard Deduction of $13,850 in 2023 – which means your kids won't pay taxes on that amount either (up to $13,850)! <u>Stop paying taxes on your income and then giving your children an allowance! Instead, pay them in pre-tax money for working for you!</u> The cherry on top is that you can now establish a Roth IRA for each child and contribute up to 100% of their earned income (with a cap of $6,500 in 2023). Your child can then withdraw 100% of the Roth IRA (both principal and growth) tax-free in retirement (after age 59 ½). Do you know who loves that outcome? Everybody but the IRS!

Okay, great, but what does this have to do with saving for college? Well, because you already paid taxes on them, Roth IRA contributions can be withdrawn at any time (for any reason). So, let's say you start now with a 10-year-old child who will head off to college in eight years. Even if Roth IRA contribution limits don't increase, you could contribute $6,500 per year to a Roth IRA (assuming your child has that much earned income) for eight years – a total of $52,000. The entire $52,000 can be withdrawn whenever you want to pay for tuition, books, room and board – whatever. There are no restrictions on how you use those funds. You can also continue to make Roth IRA contributions for the child after age 18 (again, as long as they have at least as much earned income as the amount of the contribution). Withdrawals above the amounts contributed (i.e., of earnings) would subject those additional withdrawals to taxes and early withdrawal penalties – but if you don't take out more than you've put in, you're good!

So, the Roth IRA as an education savings vehicle provides the following advantages:

- You can make larger contributions than in a Coverdell (up to $6,500/year instead of $2,000/year).

- You can self-direct and invest in just about anything you want (unlike the limited options in 529 Plans).

- If your child ends up not attending college (or not finishing), the funds are not required to be used for educational purposes. They can remain in the account and give your child a head start in saving and investing for retirement.

Stop Choosing

- **To believe the student loan myth.** <u>Repeat after me – "I DO NOT need student loans to go to college!"</u> It will take planning, saving, working, and sacrificing, but you (and your kids) can get your Bachelor's degree debt-free.

- **To enable your children.** Set firm boundaries on how (and how much) you will help financially. Set the expectation that your kids will work and save for college during high school and will hold down a job during college. They will thank you when they graduate debt-free!

- **Procrastination.** Start saving now! Actually saving is more important than how you invest those savings.

Start Choosing

- **To put on your oxygen mask first.** Don't sacrifice your current or future financial well-being to pay for your kids to go to school. Do the steps in order.

- **To weigh the costs and benefits of college (or of a particular college).** <u>College is not worth it regardless of the price!</u> Explore lower-cost alternatives to the "dream school." A degree from an in-state public school can get you just as far as one from a private school that costs four times as much. The same goes for graduate school. $250,000 in debt for a Master's Degree in Early Childhood Education (where the median pay is $49,200/year[73]) doesn't make any freaking sense!

- **To be aware of your education savings and investment alternatives.** Regardless of what Wall Street would have you

---

[73] https://www.monster.com/career-advice/article/best-and-worst-paying-masters-degrees

believe, the 529 Plan is not the only game in town. Explore the Coverdell and Roth IRA as alternatives.

9

STEP SIX - PAY OFF YOUR HOME EARLY

Nothing embodies the American dream quite like home ownership. For most of us, a home is the largest and most expensive purchase we will ever make. And unlike a vehicle, it truly is (or should be) an investment – because real estate tends to increase in value. As of 2022, roughly 66% of Americans owned their homes[74]. Of that number, about 171 million Americans borrowed money to make their home ownership dreams come true[75]. This isn't surprising. I don't know if you know this, but houses are expensive. The current average home value in the U.S. is $339,048[76]. Very few of us have that kind of cash lying around, and even financial advisors as debt-averse as Dave Ramsey are okay with borrowing money to purchase a home.

That doesn't mean the debt numbers still aren't a bit breathtaking. According to the Federal Reserve Bank of New York, Americans carried $12.01 trillion in mortgage debt as of the second quarter of 2023[77]. The average mortgage loan balance was

---

[74] https://www.statista.com/statistics/184902/homeownership-rate-in-the-us-since-2003/
[75] https://www.pewtrusts.org/en/research-and-analysis/issue-briefs/2022/04/millions-of-americans-have-used-risky-financing-arrangements-to-buy-homes
[76] https://www.zillow.com/home-values/102001/united-states/
[77] https://www.lendingtree.com/home/mortgage/u-s-mortgage-market-

about $236,000 as of September 2022[78], and the average monthly mortgage payment was $1,836[79].

Given that shelter is essential to any budget, how do we tackle the costs of putting a roof over our heads? When it comes to housing, I suggest that you remember the following "Five Don'ts":

1) **<u>Don't</u> assume that buying is always better than renting.** Regardless of the other factors involved, I do not recommend buying a home when you are already in debt. A home is only as strong as its foundation; the same goes for your finances. <u>Do not buy a home until you have built your financial foundation by completing Steps 1-3 (i.e., you are debt-free and have a fully-funded emergency fund equal to 3-6 months of household expenses)</u>. But Jarom, isn't renting just throwing away money? Not necessarily — especially if you don't plan to spend 5-8 years or more in your next place. According to a recent study, owning a home costs an average of $1,176 more per month than renting a professionally managed apartment[80]. The difference is explained by external factors (such as the fact that mortgage interest rates have doubled since early 2022 and home prices have risen more sharply than rents) and by the intrinsic differences between buying and renting. Renters don't have to worry about maintenance, repairs, property taxes, insurance, etc. To paraphrase the late, great stand-up comedian, Mitch Hedberg, I'd always rather go to the Apartment Depot than Home Depot. The Apartment Depot is a bunch of people standing around saying, 'We ain't gotta do [crap]!'

---

statistics/#Outstandingmortgages
[78] https://www.experian.com/blogs/ask-experian/how-much-americans-owe-on-their-mortgages-in-every-state/
[79] https://www.bankrate.com/mortgages/average-mortgage-debt/
[80] https://www.nmhc.org/research-insight/research-notes/2023/putting-rent-increases-into-perspective/#notes

Yes, when you own your home, you are building equity. However, that equity usually doesn't make up for the additional costs associated with home ownership until you have been in the home for five years or more. Buying a home can be amazing – but it isn't always the answer. Here is a list of pros and cons for both buying and renting.

Pros of Buying

- **You Are (Likely) Building Equity.** Each payment you make reduces the amount you owe on your mortgage. At the same time, real estate tends to increase in value over time. The difference between what your home is worth and what you owe on your mortgage is the "equity" you have in your home. Your home equity is what you would make (minus closing costs and realtor fees) if you were to sell your home. You can also borrow against the equity in your home (which we will discuss in more detail later).

- **There Are (Potential) Tax Advantages.** I'm a tax attorney – of course I'm going to talk about taxes! Uncle Sam has decided he wants to incentivize home ownership, so many of the costs of home ownership (such as property taxes and mortgage interest) are tax deductible. Sweet, right? Well, not so fast, my friend – these advantages are often oversold by people who are also trying to sell you a home. It is important to recognize that the ability to deduct these expenses only matters if you "itemize" your deductions on your taxes instead of using the "Standard Deduction." You would only choose to itemize if your total deductible expenses (like state and local income or sales taxes, property taxes, mortgage interest, and charitable contributions) are greater than the Standard Deduction offered by the IRS. In 2023, the Standard Deduction is $13,850 for Single filers and $27,700 for those who are Married Filing

Jointly[81]. Because the Standard Deduction is so high, an estimated 90% of taxpayers take it[82]. If you are in that 90%, the ability to deduct mortgage interest and property taxes does you no good. Even if you itemize, your deduction for state and local taxes (the "SALT" deduction) is capped at $10,000, so you still may not get to deduct your property taxes.

- **You Can Fix Up the Place.** Has the carpet seen better days? Do the cabinets and countertops in the kitchen give you *Brady Bunch* flashbacks? When you buy, you can change all of that (and whatever else you want). But remember, you are footing the bill for all those changes – and you have to figure out how to get them done.

- **(Unless You Choose a Condo or Townhome) You Don't Share Walls.** My wife and I lived in apartments for the first few years of our marriage. So, we know from personal experience that in an apartment, when your neighbors smoke, you smoke. When they watch TV or listen to music, you watch TV or listen to music. And when they decide to play electric guitar and drunkenly belt out Emo tunes at 3 a.m., you get an unanticipated (and unwanted) seat in the front row. Getting out of those close quarters can be a huge advantage to home ownership.

---

[81] https://www.irs.gov/newsroom/irs-provides-tax-inflation-adjustments-for-tax-year-2023
[82] https://www. https://money.cnn.com/2009/11/24/real_estate/mortgages_underwater/forbes.com/advisor/taxes/standard-deduction/

Cons of Buying

- **Real Estate Doesn't Always Appreciate (Especially in the Short Term).** It's possible to buy a home, pay the mortgage for a few years, and have it be worth less than you paid (or even less than you owe – just ask 2009[83]).

- **Your Housing-Related Expenses Will Be Higher.** Renters insurance is cheap. The average premium is $15/month[84]. Homeowners policies average about $120/month[85]. Depending on where you live, you may also need to add flood or earthquake coverage. Your utility bills will also increase when you move from a 1,000 sq. ft. apartment to a 2,000 sq. ft. house (with a yard). Oh, and don't forget about the costs (and joys) of belonging to a Homeowners Association (HOA).

- **You Will Become Very Familiar With Your Local Lowes or Home Depot.** When stuff breaks or wears out (and it will), you are on the hook to fix or replace it. If you are handy and enjoy home maintenance and repairs, this can be a source of fulfillment and joy. If, on the other hand, you're like me and the hardware store feels like a place where you don't speak the language, it can be daunting (even overwhelming). Regardless of your level of proficiency as a handyman, this responsibility can get expensive – especially when the roof starts leaking, or the HVAC system gives up the ghost.

---

[83] https://www.npr.org/sections/thetwo-way/2009/11/one_in_four_us_homes_underwate.html
[84] https://www.nerdwallet.com/article/insurance/how-much-is-renters-insurance
[85] https://www.bankrate.com/insurance/homeowners-insurance/homeowners-insurance-cost/

- **You Are Tied to the House.** That doesn't mean you can't untie yourself, but if you get transferred to a different city (or if you get an opportunity to work or study abroad for a couple of years), you will almost certainly have to sell the house or get it ready to rent (and be prepared to enjoy the "opportunities" that can come with being a landlord). It's also harder to move if you just don't like the neighborhood (or schools, or whatever).

Pros of Renting

- **Your Landlord Gets to Fix Stuff.** If you'd rather hang out at the Apartment Depot (where people stand around talking about how they don't have to do anything) than the Home Depot, renting has its advantages. On the other hand, you do have to wait for the landlord to get around to doing what you need.

- **Freedom!** If you're not ready to put down roots and are not 100% sure you want to be in the same place in 2-3 years, renting is probably for you. It's almost always easier to get out of a lease than a mortgage.

- **You Will Almost Always Save Money – In the Short Term.** Maintenance Costs? Zero. Insurance? Way cheaper. Security Deposit? A lot less than a down payment. HOA fees? Nope. Private Mortgage Insurance? What in the world is that?!

Cons of Renting

- **Rents Go Up (Mortgage Payments Don't).** Assuming your mortgage has a fixed rate (and it should), the amount you pay towards principal and interest (combined) each month will not change. Rents usually go up every year. As such, renting can be great in the short run – but it is not a long-term solution.

- **Hope You Like the Place – Because You Ain't Making Changes.** At least not without the landlord's permission. Stop thinking about that dream kitchen because you're not getting it as a renter. Your decorating choices are your only outlet for "making the place your own."

- **You're Not Building Anything.** Your rent payments don't increase your equity in the home (because the equity doesn't belong to you). Rising property values don't help you (because the appreciation doesn't belong to you). And the tax breaks are meaningless (because the deductions don't belong to you). Renting long-term can feel like running on a hamster wheel – your efforts (making rent payments) aren't getting you anywhere.

<u>My best advice when it comes to buying a home is this: slow down</u>. Buying is not always the slam dunk correct answer. Think about the pros and cons of buying and renting above. And if time is of the essence because the real estate market is just that hot, realize you're probably set up to overpay anyway. Take a step back and make sure you aren't making your decision purely out of emotion.

2) **<u>Don't</u> Choose to Be House-Poor.** "House-Poor" is simply a term that describes being in a situation where you are paying more than you can afford for housing costs. Remember, housing costs are more than just your rent or mortgage payment. They include insurance, property taxes, maintenance, repairs, and utilities. Notice that I said rent – renters can be house-poor, too.

Sometimes, becoming house-poor is (at least somewhat) out of your control. Maybe you lost your job, or your hours at work have been cut. Perhaps you've encountered an unexpected medical or vehicle expense. These are obviously difficult situations that are often beyond your control. However, choosing to walk through the steps in the correct order isn't beyond your control. If you wait to buy a home until you are otherwise debt-free and have saved 3-6 months of living expenses, a temporary change in your earnings or expenses will not turn into a crisis where you have to consider selling your home. If you rent, your fully-funded emergency fund will give you time to decide if you can weather the storm or need to start looking for cheaper places to stay.

With that being said, being house-poor is usually a result of choosing not to "pay freaking attention" to how your housing choices will affect your overall financial picture. Too many of us have the attitude that when it comes to a home, we should borrow whatever we can qualify for. While this attitude may produce a home that will wow your friends from the curb and when they walk in the front door, it will also stick you with a mortgage payment that will put a strain on your marriage and keep you from doing other things you'd like to do (without going into more debt – which is what **a lot** of Americans end up doing). It's why nearly 7 in 10 Americans say they feel house-poor[86].

To that end, I advise that you limit your monthly housing costs (including principal, interest, property taxes, homeowners insurance, private mortgage insurance (if any), and HOA dues (if any)) to 25% of your monthly take-home pay. Mr. Ramsey would also tell you to do this math based

---

[86] https://www.nasdaq.com/articles/69-of-homeowners-feel-house-poor.-did-you-buy-too-much-house

on a 15-year fixed-rate mortgage. 15-year mortgages are fantastic. They have lower interest rates and allow (more like force) you to pay off your mortgage in half the time. However, because home values tend to increase in the long run and because the longer loan term can save you hundreds of dollars each month (thereby giving you some breathing room in your budget for other financial goals), I am okay with a 30-year fixed-rate mortgage. After all, you are free to make larger mortgage payments when your budget allows. You can even choose to pay your 30-year mortgage like it's a 15-year mortgage (and dial it back to the minimum payment when life throws you some curves). <u>If you rent, this means your rent (and any other related costs like parking and pet fees) should not exceed 25% of your take-home pay</u>.

3) **<u>Don't</u> Underestimate the Costs of Homeownership.** Consider all the upfront and ongoing costs of owning a home as you decide whether to buy. Examples of additional upfront costs are:

- A deposit or down payment
- Lender fees
- Title fees
- Appraisal and inspection fees
- Escrow fees

We've discussed these previously, but ongoing costs include:

- Property taxes
- Homeowners Insurance
- Repairs
- Maintenance
- HOA fees/dues
- Private mortgage insurance (PMI)

Speaking of PMI ...

4) **<u>Don't</u> Overlook Private Mortgage Insurance (PMI).** PMI protects your lender (not you). It is there to cover the difference if you default on your mortgage, and the amount the lender receives from the sale of your home at foreclosure is not enough to cover what you owe on the loan. The vast majority of lenders require it when your down payment is less than 20% of the purchase price of the home. It can be paid upfront and be rolled into the loan, or it can be paid monthly. How much you pay will depend on the size of your loan, the amount you put down, your credit score, and other factors your lender or the Government seems to pick out of thin air. PMI is usually 0.5% to 2% of your mortgage balance per year. So, on a $300,000 mortgage, you'd be looking at a monthly PMI premium of $125-$500.

Depending on your loan type, you may be able to cancel your PMI by request when your loan balance drops below 80% of the fair market value of your home (as determined by an appraisal that you will have to pay for). <u>However, the best way to cancel PMI is not to pay for it in the first place! This is accomplished by putting down at least 20% of the purchase price of the home</u>. However, saving up a 20% down payment can be daunting for a first-time homebuyer. It may take multiple years. I am okay with first-time homebuyers putting down 5-10% - but only on a conventional loan. This leads me to my final "don't."

5) **<u>Don't</u> Take Out Anything Other Than a Fixed-Rate Conventional Loan.** A conventional loan is simply one that is not part of a specific government program[87]. Instead, conventional loans are originated, backed, and serviced by private lenders like banks and credit unions. They represent

---

[87] https://www.consumerfinance.gov/owning-a-home/loan-options/conventional-loans/

more than 80% of all home loans[88]. FHA and VA loans are the most common government mortgage programs. Let's compare them to conventional loans.

Conventional Loans

- Typically (but don't always) require at least 5% down.
- Typically require a credit score of at least 620-660[89].
- Usually have the lowest interest rates – and the rates just get lower the more you put down and the better your credit.
- Require private mortgage insurance (PMI) if you put down less than 20%. However, you can cancel PMI once you have at least 20% equity in your home (usually because property values have increased and/or you have renovated the home and increased its value).

FHA Loans

The Fair Housing Administration (FHA) administers a program that encourages home ownership by making mortgage loans available to first-time home buyers and people who don't have the credit or down payment to qualify for a conventional loan. Because these are the folks most likely to default on a mortgage, these loans are guaranteed by the FHA. Here is what to know about FHA loans:

- They are only offered by certain "FHA-approved" lenders willing to jump through the necessary government hoops.
- You can get one with as little as 3.5% down.
- Your credit score can be as low as 580 (if you only put

---

[88] https://www.moneygeek.com/mortgage/conventional-loan/
[89] https://www.experian.com/blogs/ask-experian/what-is-a-conventional-loan/

down 3.5%). If you can put down 10%, your score can be as low as 500.

- You'll pay a mortgage insurance premium (MIP) of 1.75% of your mortgage balance upfront (usually, it's rolled into your loan). On a $300,000 mortgage, that's $5,250. You also get to pay an annual MIP of 0.45-1.05 of your average annual loan balance. Assuming a mid-range annual MIP of 0.75%, that's another $2,250/year (or $187.50/month). <u>Unlike PMI on a conventional loan, MIPs never go away on an FHA loan – unless you put 10% down. In that case, it drops off after 11 years</u>[90] <u>(because it's the government, and 10 years would have been too easy to remember)</u>.

<u>VA Loans</u>

The Department of Veterans Affairs (VA) administers this program. It offers mortgage loans to active-duty members of the military, as well as veterans and their surviving spouses. Here is the low-down on VA loans:

- They are only offered by certain "VA-approved" lenders willing to jump through the necessary government hoops.
- One significant "advantage" is that you can get a VA loan with nothing down. Sounds incredible, right? Well, be careful. <u>Walking into a home purchase with no equity can be scary. If the housing market (nationally or locally) dips, you will quickly end up with a home worth less than you owe. And remember, no one ever drowns unless they are underwater.</u>
- Interest rates tend to be similar to (or even slightly better) than those on conventional mortgages for 30-year loans. On 15-year loans, the rates tend not to be as

---

[90] https://www.ramseysolutions.com/real-estate/what-is-an-fha-loan

good as conventional mortgages.
- The VA program itself has no minimum credit score requirement (although the lender might).
- They carry a "funding fee" of 1.25% to 3.3%. If you put less than 5% down, the fee will either be 2.15% (if this is your first VA loan) or 3.3% (if you've used a VA loan before[91]). On a $300,000 mortgage, that's either $6,450 or $9,900 you'll need to pay in cash at closing or roll into your loan. If you're putting down 0% and rolling the funding fee into your mortgage, you are starting your homeownership adventure underwater – not a great start.
- You can get approved with a higher debt-to-income ratio. However, because you've read this book and you're choosing not to be house-poor, this "benefit" doesn't mean much to you.

As you can see, a conventional loan is the way to go. The other type of mortgage to beware of is the variable or adjustable-rate mortgage (ARM). ARMs offer lower rates for an initial period (five years in the most common type of ARM). After that, the rate adjusts each year for the remaining term of the loan (typically 30 years total), depending on where interest rates are at the time. ARMs are commonly used by folks who want to "afford" a more expensive home. Often, it only serves to delay the inevitability of becoming house-poor.

But Jarom, what if I can't qualify for a conventional mortgage (or afford the payment on the house I want on a conventional mortgage without being house-poor)? Let me shoot you straight – because the mortgage guy probably won't. It means you shouldn't buy a home (or at least you

---

[91] https://www.va.gov/housing-assistance/home-loans/funding-fee-and-closing-costs/

shouldn't buy *that* home). Don't let your emotions get the best of you, and don't let yourself become infected with a case of the "I wants." There's nothing wrong with waiting. Keep working your plan. Save up a bigger down payment (maybe even 20% or more to avoid PMI). Take steps to improve your credit. The wait will be worth it when you own your home (instead of it owning you), and home ownership is a blessing (instead of a curse).

Ok, you've been intentional about buying a home. You didn't pull the trigger until you were debt-free. Or, if you did things out of order (like I did), you worked your tail off to become debt-free other than your mortgage. Now, it's time to pay off your mortgage early. Lots of folks on YouTube and TikTok will say you shouldn't. Here's why they're wrong:

- **It will save you tens of thousands (maybe even hundreds of thousands) in interest.** For a $300,000 loan on a 30-year conventional fixed-rate loan at 6.5%, you will pay about $682,000 in principal and interest over the life of the loan. If you pay an extra $717 each month, you will pay it off in 15 years and pay about $470,000 in principal and interest – a savings of $212,000. That is $212,000 that can be invested, spent, and given away (to someone other than the bank).

- **It brings peace.** Perhaps you'll indulge me a bit while I quote Gordon B. Hinckley, a former President of the Church of Jesus Christ of Latter-day Saints. In a 1998 address to the Church, he recounted the following, including an anecdote about one of his counselors at the time (President James E. Faust):

    What a wonderful feeling it is to be free of debt, to have a little money against a day of emergency put away where it can be retrieved when necessary.

President Faust would not tell you this himself. Perhaps I can tell it, and he can take it out on me afterward. He had a mortgage on his home, drawing four percent interest. Many people would have told him he was foolish to pay off that mortgage when it carried so low a rate of interest. But the first opportunity he had to acquire some means, he and his wife determined they would pay off their mortgage. He has been free of debt since that day. That's why he wears a smile on his face, and that's why he whistles while he works[92].

A paid-off home mortgage will lower your blood pressure. It will improve your relationships with your spouse and children. It will give you the financial freedom to do things (or not do things) you never thought were possible. It will unlock a streak of generosity inside you that you never knew was there.

It's not just Gordon B. Hinckley and Dave Ramsey (and me) who believe it makes sense to pay off your mortgage as soon as possible. Here are a few additional thoughts on mortgages from other financial experts:

"There's never an incentive to stay in debt. Life is unpredictable. What happens if you're laid off or incur unexpected expenses elsewhere? Your once-manageable mortgage is suddenly going to seem not-so-manageable[93]." – **Kevin O'Leary (Entrepreneur, Financier, and Panelist on *Shark Tank*)**.

"More than one in three homeowners 65 or older is still paying off a mortgage. This is so not okay. If you plan on remaining in your home through your golden years, you should make it your top

---

[92] https://www.churchofjesuschrist.org/study/general-conference/1998/10/to-the-boys-and-to-the-men?lang=eng
[93] https://www.cnbc.com/2018/06/13/kevin-oleary-pay-off-your-mortgage-by-this-age.html

priority right now to get the mortgage paid off before you retire. You will be more protected from any number of unknowns: being forced to leave your job sooner than you expected; or the possibility that tax rates will rise, effectively reducing the value of what you have saved in your traditional retirement accounts; or the risk that investment returns will disappoint[94]." – **Suze Orman (Financial Advisor, Author, and Television and Podcast Host).**

"I can tell you, having been a financial advisor at Morgan Stanley, my clients who retired at 50 years old, the secret was: They had paid their mortgage off early[95]." – **David Bach (financial author, television personality, motivational speaker, entrepreneur and founder of FinishRich.com).**

However, as I noted earlier, not everyone agrees that paying off your mortgage early is a good idea. The argument on the other side is that if the interest rate on your mortgage is low (which has been the case for the past decade or more), you should only make the minimum payments. Then, instead of taking excess cash and throwing it at the mortgage, you should take that cash and invest it (in the stock market, other real estate, etc.). The thinking is that the rate of return on your investments will be better than the interest you save when paying off your mortgage early. This is what they mean by "making the spread."

Let me be the first to say that the math of this concept absolutely can work. If your mortgage is at 4% interest and your investments return 10%, you will come out ahead. However, the flaw in this plan is all the "ifs." The concept works:

---

[94] https://www.cnbc.com/2017/11/14/suze-orman-pay-off-your-mortgage-before-you-retire.html
[95] https://www.cnbc.com/2018/03/09/david-bach-buying-a-home-can-help-you-retire-early.html

- <u>If</u> you take the cash and invest all of it. This takes a measure of discipline that not everyone possesses. Plenty of folks end up spending the excess cash instead of investing it.

- <u>If</u> your investments perform well. <u>Fun fact: investments can decrease in value.</u> In 2022, the Dow lost almost 9%, the S&P was down more than 19%, and the Nasdaq gave away nearly one-third of its value. When you make additional payments on your mortgage, you know the rate of return on your investment before you make it. It's the interest rate on your loan. Your return is certain. I don't know about you, but I like certainty!

- <u>If</u> you sell at the right time. Paper gains are just that – only on paper. Many people hang on too long or sell too soon, so they never end up reaping the benefit of their "gains."

- <u>If</u> you don't lose too much to taxes. The profits from selling an investment are taxed at a rate of 15%-37% (depending on how long you hold the investment and how much total income you make for the year). Oh, and that's just federal. Don't forget about state-level taxes! In all but seven states, you'll pay those, too (at a rate above 10% in places like California, New York, New Jersey, and Washington D.C.[96]).

While we're on the subject of taxes, please let me take some time to debunk one of the dumbest pieces of financial advice I've heard. It goes like this: "Be careful about paying off your mortgage early because you'll lose the mortgage interest deduction on your taxes." <u>My response to this advice is only three words: "Who freaking cares?!"</u>

Let's go ahead and set aside the fact that most people don't itemize their deductions (which is the only way the mortgage

---

[96] https://www.realized1031.com/capital-gains-tax-rate

interest deduction would matter) because if you take the standard deduction, the amount you pay in mortgage interest is irrelevant to your tax liability. I will gladly assume that John (the fictional person receiving this terrible advice) does itemize. I am also willing to set the facts as advantageously as possible for the person dispensing the advice, so let's also assume that John is easily in the highest federal tax bracket (37%). Let's also say that John pays $10,000/year in mortgage interest. This means he gets a $10,000 tax deduction. Because he pays taxes at the 37% rate, that deduction saves John an impressive $3,700 in taxes ($10,000 x 0.37). Sweet, right? Well, let's keep going.

If John completely pays off his mortgage by the end of the year, he will lose that $10,000 deduction, which means he will pay $3,700 more in taxes next year (which I will admit does suck). However, he will also pay his mortgage lender $10,000 less in interest – so he's still $6,300 ahead. If John is in the 22% tax bracket, he would only lose $2,200 in tax savings, so he'd come out $7,800 ahead. And (again) because most people don't itemize their deductions, John is probably ahead by the entire $10,000. <u>John can now take that extra cash and invest it. He is both debt-free and has extra money available to make investments. Hence, keeping a mortgage around just to keep the tax deduction on the interest makes no sense whatsoever.</u>

Investing the cash you would otherwise use to pay down your mortgage (and making the spread) sounds intelligent and sophisticated. It sounds like what the smart guy would do. It's the type of thing you can impress people with at parties. But here's the thing – I don't go to parties (if I can help it). When someone does drag me to a party, my goal is to get out of there as quickly as possible. I give zero [freaks] about what the people there think of me. I like simplicity, certainty, and security. Paying off my mortgage early checks all those boxes.

With all of that being said, I also like transparency. In the interest of transparency, I need to disclose that although I typically have extra cash each month after saving for retirement and education, I am not currently throwing that cash at my mortgage. I am instead saving it to renovate/add on to my home and purchase new vehicles without taking on any debt. Making sure I don't borrow money for a new car is more important to me than making progress on my mortgage, and paying down the mortgage just to turn around and borrow money for the home renovation/addition doesn't make sense. Situations where you may only make minimum mortgage payments for a time include:

- Saving for home renovations or a down payment on a new home.
- Saving to pay cash for a new vehicle.
- Saving to cash flow additional education.
- Saving to cover out-of-pocket expenses for a new baby or other expected medical costs.
- Saving to make cash investments in a new or existing business (instead of financing them through debt).
- Saving to pay cash or make a significant down payment for an investment property.

Paying off your mortgage early is a worthy financial goal and an essential step in obtaining financial peace. It should not be ignored or skipped. In fact, according to the most extensive study of millionaires ever conducted, about two-thirds of all millionaires live in a paid-for home[97]. However, as you can see, it's sort of what you do "after you've done everything else." <u>That doesn't mean you don't have a deadline – my goal is that no one who reads this book is still making mortgage payments when they retire. There is no peace in that.</u>

---

[97] https://www.ramseysolutions.com/retirement/how-to-go-from-zero-to-millionaire

As you make payments to reduce your mortgage balance and as your home appreciates, your financial equity in your home will continue to rise. At the same time, most of us also become emotionally attached to our homes. It's where we've made memories with our families. It's where our kids grew up. This "emotional equity" should not be underestimated. Unlike a vehicle, a home truly is a financial and emotional investment, and it makes sense to take reasonable steps to protect it from potential lawsuits. Here is a list of some of the most common ones:

1. **Take advantage of your state's "homestead exemption."** The homestead exemption is an amount of equity in your personal residence that is exempt from the claims of creditors. Some states (like Florida and Texas) have unlimited homestead exemptions. Others (like New Jersey and Pennsylvania) have none. Most states have one, and they can vary from $10,000, all the way up to several hundred thousand dollars. Some states require a filing to claim the exemption. Others don't. Learn the rules in your state and take whatever action is necessary to get the exemption (regardless of your level of equity).

2. **Look into "tenancy by the entirety."** Tenancy by the entirety is a form of shared/joint property ownership that permits spouses to own property as a single legal entity. It is only available to legally married couples. When a property is held this way, a creditor with a judgment against just one spouse is restricted from seizing the property. This is a great option when one spouse has a high-liability job (doctor, dentist, lawyer, engineer, etc.) and the other doesn't. Unfortunately, it is only available in about half of the states.

3. **Do some "equity stripping."** Equity stripping is the process of placing one or more liens against your own property so it looks like the property has less equity than it does. True equity stripping could involve taking out a home

equity line of credit (HELOC) and actually borrowing against that line of credit (perhaps to purchase investments). The HELOC lender then records a second mortgage against the home in the total amount of the line of credit. In such a situation, a new creditor would only be able to get at what remains from the sales proceeds of the home after selling costs are paid, the first and second mortgage holders are made whole, and the homeowner receives any applicable homestead exemption. Because I don't like the idea of borrowing against your home to make investments, I don't advocate for true equity stripping.

However, it is possible to obtain a HELOC and not borrow against the line of credit. When you do, the HELOC lender will record the same second mortgage against the property. This mortgage will appear in any asset/title search and make it look like the home has much less equity than it actually does. This could dissuade a potential plaintiff from deciding to sue you in the first place. If you don't qualify for a HELOC from a bank or a credit union, you could instead form an LLC in a "privacy" state (like Wyoming or New Mexico) where very little information about the LLC is disclosed publicly and have that LLC record a "friendly lien" against your home. The unused HELOC and the friendly lien would be sliced up like a hot knife through butter in the event of an actual lawsuit, but they can help keep a lawsuit from happening.

4. **Think about a Domestic Asset Protection Trust (DAPT).** A DAPT is simply a trust set up under the laws of a particular state (twenty states currently have a DAPT statute) that shields the trust's assets from the liabilities of the trust's beneficiaries. DAPTs can cost $2,000 - $2,500 and involve jumping through various hoops, so they should not be entered into without speaking with an expert first. However, under specific parameters, they can provide

incredible asset protection benefits.

Stop Choosing

- **To believe that renting is always dumb.** There are plenty of situations where renting makes sense. Just because you can buy a house doesn't mean you should!

- **To pay mortgage insurance.** Let me get this straight. I pay the mortgage insurance premiums, and if there's a problem and I default, the insurance policy pays the lender – not me? Hard pass.

- **To be house-poor.** A bigger, newer home with better countertops is great – as long as you can afford it! Make sure your mortgage payment (including property taxes, insurance, and mortgage insurance (if any)) is less than 25% of your monthly take-home pay.

Start Choosing

- **A guaranteed return (in the form of interest savings).** Don't play the "arbitrage" game where you invest the extra money you would otherwise use to pay down your mortgage, hoping to earn more than your interest rate.

- **Mortgage loans without acronyms.** The government loves acronyms – and at the end of the day, FHA, VA, USDA, and other alphabet soup loans are government programs. Conventional loans are always your best bet. They keep mortgage insurance at bay and have fewer strings and better terms than government loans.

- **The <u>peace</u> that comes from a life without a house payment.** Don't underestimate what having this weight off your shoulders (and your mind) will mean to you!

10

STEP SEVEN – BUILD WEALTH AND BE GENEROUS!

This is where things get fun! You've worked yourself free of all non-mortgage debt (and you've decided you're never going back). You are saving about 15% of your income for retirement. You're saving for your children's college education (if applicable). You have either paid off your mortgage or are working on it. Walking through these steps (especially if you've tossed the weight of your mortgage off your back) has freed up what Mr. Ramsey calls "your most powerful wealth-building tool" – your income.

When you don't have monthly payments to worry about (or maybe just one), you will end up with extra money at the end of the month. What a concept, right? That means you will need to decide what to do with that money. All your options can be boiled down to three basic choices:

- **Spend it.**
- **Give it away.**
- **Invest it.**

Guess what? You should do all three – and now is not the time to stop being intentional. Budget for what you plan to spend, give away, and invest each month. Make plans to save towards big goals in each area, and stick to those plans. If you're not paying any freaking attention, you'll find none of the three areas are turning out as successful or satisfying as you had hoped. Let's explore these three areas for a moment.

Spending

I want to take a few moments to speak not only in defense <u>but in praise</u> of spending. <u>Spending money (in and of itself) is not wrong. It is not immoral. Spending money you don't have is</u>. When you are in Step 7, you should not be afraid to spend more (maybe significantly more) than you did in Steps 1-3. One of the reasons you sacrificed to be able to win with money was so you could <u>enjoy the money!</u>

You earned that money – go ahead and spend it! Drop $15,000 (in cash, of course) on that two-week trip to the South Pacific that would have been beyond stupid when you were neck-deep in credit card and car debt. Commit $35,000 (in cash, of course) to upgrade out of that 2009 Toyota Prius (as long as it doesn't push the value of your vehicles (including boats and other toys) over 50% of your annual income). Take your spouse to a (very) nice restaurant every once in a while. Go a little crazy for your kids! Buy them a golf cart to tool around the neighborhood. Spend a little extra to get them really sweet bikes for Christmas. Put a trampoline in the ground in the backyard.

<u>All these things are great – as long as you are still being intentional</u>. Set your limits and stay within them. Don't be flashy or showy. Don't buy a brand-new car (and vacuum up all the depreciation) until you are a net-worth millionaire. Don't forget about giving and investing. But also, please don't feel guilty about spending! If you do, remember this – your consumer spending stimulates the economy! You're doing your patriotic duty!

Giving

Think for a minute about what being in Step 7 means. <u>It means you are self-reliant in your finances</u>. No one needs to check in on you and your family to see if you have enough in your pantry or if your kids will be getting anything for Christmas. Because you don't have to focus all your attention and energy inward to make sure you have enough to pay your rent or cover gas and groceries this week, you can look outward. Your head is well above the water, so you can see the people in your neighborhood and community who may be struggling to stay afloat.

You notice the stressed-out mother of four behind you in line at Wal-Mart, and you tell the cashier to run your card for her groceries as well. You have the financial freedom to tip the college student who provided you with excellent service at dinner an extra $100. When the neighbor you exercise with every morning confides in you that her family is having trouble making ends meet, you can help without thinking twice. You're able to support causes you believe in on both a local and a global scale. Because you're not strapped financially, you also have time to volunteer for those causes. You get to make a difference in the lives of people near and far. To get a bit philosophical or religious, being in Step 7 means you've put yourself in a position where God can use you as an instrument to bless the lives of his other children. When you can bless others in this way, the blessings come back to you tenfold!

Don't believe me on that whole "blessings coming back to you" thing? Consider this:

- Spending money on others can reduce your blood pressure just as significantly as medication and exercise[98].

---

[98] https://theconversation.com/want-to-do-something-good-for-your-health-try-being-generous-51084

- Depression rates are more than 20% lower in people who give away more than 10% of their incomes than in the rest of the population[99].
- Generosity reduces stress[100].
- Being generous with your time can extend your life. One study found that people who volunteered for two or more causes had a 63% lower rate of mortality than people who didn't volunteer during the study period[101].

Simply put, being generous (with both your time and money) is good for you. Please don't leave it out of the equation when you think about how to build true wealth.

Investing

From a numbers perspective, Americans build wealth by investing – plain and simple. Please understand that I am not here to tell you what to invest in. That is not my role. I give financial advice – not investment advice. My best financial advice when you are at this point in your journey is this: You need to invest! Maybe that means taking a run at the stock market. Perhaps cryptocurrency's your thing. Maybe you want to get into real estate or start your own business. Perhaps it's all of the above. Whatever it is, it's time to do it!

Ok, then, how should you invest? Warren Buffett (perhaps the most famous investor in American history) has some investment rules you may want to be aware of: "Rule No. 1 is never lose money. Rule No. 2 is never forget Rule No. 1." Easy, right?! Undoubtedly, almost all investing carries some risk of loss. What

---

[99] https://newrepublic.com/article/119477/science-generosity-why-giving-makes-you-happy
[100] https://www.sciencedaily.com/releases/2014/10/141028101625.htm
[101] https://health.usnews.com/health-news/health-wellness/articles/2015/05/01/what-generosity-does-to-your-brain-and-life-expectancy

Mr. Buffett is saying is that one of the best ways to make a profit when investing is to avoid exposing yourself to losses. This makes sense because when you avoid losses, you will have more money invested, and you can compound your gains even more quickly.

One way to avoid losses would be to keep everything in a savings account. Unfortunately, that won't do the trick (even in a high-yield account that pays 4-5% interest). The reason is simple: inflation. <u>As you run around trying to build wealth, inflation is always chasing you – and inflation is relentless. Just like interest, it doesn't sleep, it doesn't take a day off, and it doesn't play favorites</u>. To outrun inflation, your investments will need to appreciate faster than the inflation rate (the rate at which each dollar loses its buying power).

Here is an example. In 2022, annual inflation ended up at 6.5%[102]. This means that, on average, one dollar could purchase 6.5% less in goods and services on December 31, 2022, than on January 1, 2022. During that same timeframe, even the highest-yield savings accounts weren't paying much more than 4% in annual interest. Therefore, even though you might have finished 2022 with about $10,400 in your savings account if you started the year with $10,000, that $10,400 would have less power to purchase goods and services on December 31 than the $10,000 did on January 1.

<u>To be clear, I am not saying that savings accounts don't have their place</u>. As we discussed in Chapter 6, they are an excellent choice for where to keep your Emergency Fund. They are also the place to save up for purchases you will make in the short term (like the new vehicle and home renovations I am saving for). Because deposits are FDIC-insured (up to $250,000), they are essentially risk-free. The funds are also easily accessible when needed, and the

---

[102] https://www.cnbc.com/2023/01/12/heres-the-inflation-breakdown-for-december-2022-in-one-chart.html

interest you earn is better than what you would get with cash sitting in a safe in your house (i.e., nada). But savings accounts do not build wealth – because they are not investments (or at least not very effective ones).

So, what qualifies as an "investment?" Let's start by defining the term. An investment is "the outlay of money usually for income or profit." I think that helps explain why a savings account isn't an investment. We don't (or shouldn't) put money in a savings account to make a profit. We park it there to maintain availability, eliminate risk, and keep up with inflation (to the extent possible).

As discussed in Chapter 7, the first place you will invest is in your retirement account(s). Investing about 15% of your income in retirement accounts like your employer 401k or a Roth IRA is Step 4. Your retirement accounts are incredible, tax-advantaged ways to build wealth. Here in Step 7, you will return to investing, but please don't forget about your retirement accounts. If the 15% you invest in Step 4 does not max out your potential retirement account contributions, you should consider going back to those accounts because of the tax advantages they provide.

Let's go through a typical scenario. Suppose Adam is 35, single with no kids, and makes $100,000/year as a W-2 employee. In Step 4, he would save/invest $15,000/year towards retirement. Adam has a 401k at work, and he is comfortable with the investment options in the plan, so he contributes $15,000/year to a Roth account there. His employer matches Adam's contributions dollar-for-dollar up to 5% of his salary.

After spending and giving away what he wants, Adam consistently ends up with an extra $500/month ($6,000/year) that he wants to invest. Because we've assumed that Adam is happy with his employer's 401k investment options, it could make sense for him to take that $500/month and throw it in his Roth 401k at work. He can make an extra $6,000 in contributions because the

401k employee contribution limit for folks under age 50 is $22,500 (and the additional $6,000 takes his total 401k contribution to $21,000). Adam won't get any extra money from his employer, and the additional contributions won't save him anything in taxes now. However, he can withdraw all the principal and growth of his Roth 401k investments tax-free once he reaches age 59 ½.

Now, let's change the scenario a bit. Bob is also 35, single with no kids, and makes $100,000/year as a W-2 employee. Just like Adam, Bob would save/invest $15,000/year towards retirement in Step 4. Bob also has a 401k at work, and the employer match at the two employers is identical. However, Bob isn't crazy about his investment options at work. Bob wants to self-direct as much of his retirement as possible into non-stock market assets. Bob should do the following:

1) Contribute $5,000 to his Roth 401k at work. His employer will match that contribution dollar-for-dollar. That's an immediate 100% return on investment. You take that seven days a week (and twice on Sunday).

2) Open a self-directed Roth IRA (at a self-directed IRA custodian like Directed IRA) and contribute the maximum amount ($6,500 in 2023) there.

3) Come back to his Roth 401k at work and contribute an additional $3,500.

$5,000 + $6,500 + $3,500 = $15,000 – so Bob is fulfilling his obligations under Step 4. But, just like Adam, Bob has an extra $500/month ($6,000/year) that he wants to invest. What should he do? Like Adam, Bob could put it in his Roth 401k at work. He has the room to do so. However, we've established that Bob doesn't like his investment choices there. The other issue with making more investments in retirement accounts is that they are trickier to access than other investments. Early withdrawals can be subject to taxes and penalties of an additional 10%. Because of that, Bob may very well choose to invest his $6,000/year outside of his retirement accounts. If Adam values being able to access these assets before retirement penalty-free, he might do the same.

Regardless of whether you do it inside or outside retirement accounts (or both), true wealth in America is built through investing, and there are two primary vehicles to do it: the Stock Market and Real Estate.

Stock Market Investments

As of the end of 2022, the total value of the U.S. Stock Market was about 40.5 Trillion dollars ($40,511,838,800,000), which was actually down more than 20% from the previous year[103]. The technical term for this is "a lot of money." Ok, how exactly can we invest in the stock market (again, either inside or outside of retirement)? While there are dozens (maybe hundreds) of ways people invest in the Stock Market, let's focus on three of the most popular:

1) **Single-Stock Investing.** This is when you make your own choices about what company or companies you will invest in and how much you will invest in each one. Being successful in single-stock investing takes more than an investment of money. It also requires time and brain power to do the necessary research to make intelligent investment decisions. It's also riskier because you tend to have your eggs in fewer baskets than by investing in mutual funds, and the fewer the number of stocks, the riskier it is. It's like playing individual numbers on the roulette wheel. Because of the risks, single stocks generally don't make sense in retirement accounts. If you want to dabble in them in taxable brokerage accounts, I would limit them to 10% of such investments.

---

[103] https://siblisresearch.com/data/us-stock-market-value/

2) **Index Mutual Funds.** First, "a mutual fund is a company that pools money from many investors and invests the money in securities such as stocks, bonds, and short-term debt. The combined holdings of the mutual fund are known as its portfolio. Investors buy shares in mutual funds. Each share represents an investor's part ownership in the fund and the income it generates[104]." Index funds are mutual funds that seek to track the returns of a particular market index, such as the S&P 500, the Dow Jones Industrials, or the Nasdaq[105]. The advantages of index funds are diversification and (usually) lower fees than the actively managed mutual funds we will discuss below. When you invest in index funds, you are essentially investing in the stock market itself. When that particular index is up, you're up. When it's down, you're down.

Index funds don't try to "beat the market" because they are "the market." Warren Buffett has said, "If you like spending six to eight hours per week working on investments, do it. If you don't, then dollar-cost average into index funds[106]." Dollar-cost averaging is the practice of investing a consistent amount at regular intervals. Combining dollar-cost averaging, index funds, and patience can be powerful. For example, if you had started investing $500/month in an S&P 500 index fund in May 2003, then by May 2023, you would have invested a total of $120,000 ($6,000/year for 20 years). <u>Your $120,000 investment would be worth more than $375,000[107]! This is true even though the S&P 500 lost 37%</u>

---

[104] https://www.investor.gov/introduction-investing/investing-basics/investment-products/mutual-funds-and-exchange-traded-1
[105] https://www.investor.gov/introduction-investing/investing-basics/investment-products/mutual-funds-and-exchange-traded-4
[106] https://www.bankrate.com/investing/warren-buffett-top-investment-advice/
[107] https://www.fool.com/investing/2023/05/09/if-you-invested-500-in-the-sp-500-every-month-for/

of its value in 2008 – its worst year since 1931.

3) **Actively Managed Mutual Funds.** As the name suggests, these are mutual funds actively managed by a fund manager or a management team. Instead of tracking a particular index, these funds rely on the fund managers to pick a mix of stocks, bonds, and other securities to try and outperform that index. The results are mixed at best – especially over the long term[108]. The fees are the other significant difference between index and actively managed funds. This may surprise you, but Wall Street fund managers don't work for free, and the cost of paying their salaries is passed on to investors. On average, the fees in actively managed funds are more than ten times higher than those of index funds[109]. Those fees suck out much of the earning power of your investments, so for an actively-managed fund to be worth it, it needs to outperform the market by enough to make up for the additional fees. Studies show that such funds are rare indeed. Less than 10% of actively managed funds outperformed the S&P 500 over the ten-year period that ended December 31, 2022[110].

There are other stock market products out there (known as "derivatives'), but just about all of them bear a striking resemblance to gambling. The most common type of derivative is stock options. An option is a contract that creates an agreement between two parties to have the option to sell or buy the stock at some point in the future at a specified price. That price is known as the "strike price" or "exercise price." I don't intend to explore options fully here other than to say that they are typically not a great long-term

---

[108] https://www.nytimes.com/2022/12/02/business/stock-market-index-funds.html
[109] https://www.forbes.com/advisor/investing/index-funds-vs-mutual-funds/
[110] https://www.forbes.com/advisor/investing/index-funds-vs-mutual-funds/

wealth-building strategy. When I worked at Charles Schwab before law school, someone told me that "options are a great way to become a millionaire – if you start out as a billionaire." Almost twenty years later, those words ring true.

Real Estate Investments

First, please be aware that we are talking about real estate investments other than your personal residence (covered in Chapter 9). The most common real estate investment is rental properties. Census data estimates that there are nearly 20 million rental properties containing more than 48 million rental units. About one-third of American households live in rental housing, and the average monthly rent surpassed $2,000 in June 2022[111]. The same data set indicates that about 70% of rental properties are owned by individual investors. However, there are many flavors of rental properties, including:

- **Long-term residential rentals.** These are properties where the renters live in the property on a long-term basis and typically enter into leases of 6-12 months or longer. The renter almost always furnishes these properties.

- **Medium (or mid-term) residential rentals.** Fully-furnished properties where the typical renter stays in the property for 30-90 days (or possibly more). The typical mid-term renter is a traveling or remote professional in healthcare, technology, construction, engineering, education, or another industry. Corporate America also rents properties medium-term to provide temporary and relocation housing to employees.

---

[111] https://www.bankrate.com/mortgages/investment-property-statistics/#tips

- **Short-term (vacation) rentals.** These are fully furnished properties where the renter is usually on vacation, and the typical stay is two weeks or less.

- **Commercial rentals.** Properties used for commercial functions like retail storefronts or office space for employees.

Regardless of the type of property involved, there are four primary ways that rental real estate investments can help build wealth:

1) **Cash Flow.** When the monthly rental income from a property is greater than the expenses related to the property (i.e., maintenance, repairs, property management fees, HOA dues, mortgage payments, etc.), the property is said to be "cash-flowing." This cash flow is an additional source of income for the property owner.

2) **Tax Benefits.** <u>The beauty of rental real estate is that the cash flow owners receive is often tax-free</u>. This is because, in addition to the actual "cash" expenses mentioned above (maintenance, repairs, mortgage interest, etc.), rental owners are also able to write off the "non-cash" expense of the "depreciation" of the building itself. This is true even though the property is usually actually **increasing** in value. Often, the allowable depreciation expense will not only wipe out all the cash flow rental income (making that income tax-free), it will allow the owner to show a "paper loss" on the property. That loss can be carried forward to offset any gain when the property is sold. Or, with the help of a skilled tax attorney or CPA, some rental owners may be able to use the loss to offset ordinary income (from a W-2 job or a small business). This can be a valuable strategy because that type of income is generally taxed at a higher rate than the capital gain income from the sale of real estate.

Also, when you hold a rental property for a year or longer, you pay "long-term capital gains" tax rates on the profit from the sale. That rate is either 0%, 15%, or 20% at the federal level (depending on your overall income), whereas "ordinary" income tax rates (on W-2 employment income or income from the operation of a business) can be as high as 37% at the federal level. <u>Also, if you plan to sell one or more rental properties and use the proceeds to invest in one or more replacement rental properties, Section 1031 of the tax code allows you to defer paying taxes on the sale proceeds (a "1031 Exchange")</u>. You can do this as many times as you'd like, and if you "swap 'til you drop," meaning you keep doing it until you die, your heirs will get a "stepped-up basis" on the properties they inherit. This means when they sell the properties, they will only pay taxes on the difference between the sales price and the fair market value of the properties on the day you pass away. <u>So, if they sell relatively soon after you pass, they will pay little or nothing in tax on the sale proceeds (which means all (or almost all) of the appreciation over all those years would be tax-free)</u>.

3) **Appreciation.** It's not exactly a show-stopping statement, but real estate tends to increase in value. This increase is called "appreciation." The increase in the value of your real estate increases your net worth. Appreciated properties can be sold, and the sales proceeds can be used for more spending, giving, and investing.

4) **Mortgage Pay Down.** Often, investors will borrow money to purchase rental real estate. When they do so, they will use the rental proceeds to make the monthly mortgage payments. As they make payments, the mortgage balance decreases. As with appreciation, the decreasing mortgage balance increases the investor's "equity" in the property. Equity is simply the difference between the fair market value of the property and what (if anything) you owe on the

property.

Ok. Let's address the elephant in the room. Most responsible financial pundits and advisors agree that no one should think about investing (in stocks or real estate) until they have built a solid financial foundation by eliminating all consumer and student debt and saving a 3-6 month emergency fund. But this is where there are diverging schools of thought. The Robert Kiyosaki faction (*Rich Dad, Poor Dad*) essentially says to load up on as much mortgage debt as possible to obtain as much investment real estate as possible (i.e., "leverage" your cash investment as much as possible) to maximize cash flow and appreciation. The Dave Ramsey faction says you only buy investment properties with cash (i.e., no leverage at all) to minimize risk.

As you know by now, I tend to fall on the Ramsey side of things. However, I don't follow Mr. Ramsey strictly here. I also don't believe in "maximizing leverage." <u>I think there is a common sense middle ground that will allow real estate investors to take advantage of leverage to build wealth in real estate without sacrificing financial peace</u>. Here are my guidelines for borrowing money to purchase rental real estate investments:

- **Do your homework.** In the legal world, we call this due diligence. We have tools to help our clients analyze whether a rental is a good investment. Investing just to invest is never a good strategy.

- **Think about taxation.** Rental properties can be depreciated over time. The costs to travel to check on a rental, make repairs, speak with tenants, property managers, etc., are business expenses that you can use to offset your rental income. So, maybe you should consider buying rentals in places you will travel to (i.e., where your parents or kids live or where you like to vacation). Now, at least some of your travel expenses are a tax deduction.

- **Put down at least 40% of the purchase price of the property in actual cash – not money you borrowed from somewhere else.** Lenders typically require you to put down 20% of the purchase price to avoid mortgage insurance. One thing I know about banks is that they have figured out what terms will provide them the most security while allowing them to suck the maximum amount of money from you in interest. Therefore, <u>I want you to be at least twice as careful as the lenders require</u>. This will provide additional security if you need to sell quickly and minimize what you send out in interest payments. The down payment should be cash you have saved, not that you borrowed from a line of credit (or from your rich uncle).

- **Don't use a HELOC or home equity loan on your primary residence to purchase a rental property.** Doing so puts your home at risk if your tenant doesn't pay (or if tenants are hard to come by). Don't put yourself in that position.

- **Have a cash contingency fund of 3-6 months of expenses related to the property.** Notice, I didn't say to build this as you go. I said to have it. It should be in place from the beginning.

Following these guidelines will allow you to use real estate to build wealth without sacrificing financial peace.

Another major potential issue with real estate investments is that they come with potential liabilities that stock market investments do not. No one slips and falls on a mutual fund investment or accuses it of breaching a contract. Those things happen to real estate investors all the time. Of course, all property owners should have insurance that will kick in when there is a problem. However, we all know that insurance companies look for reasons to deny claims whenever they can, and sometimes you may incur a judgment that exceeds your insurance policy limits even when the claim is covered.

This is why we suggest investors own their rental properties through a limited liability company (LLC) structure. Why? Let's go through an example.

Scenario 1

Let's say you buy a rental property in Colorado and decide to title it in your name. The rental income goes into your personal bank account, and you pay expenses related to the property (insurance, property taxes, maintenance and repairs, etc.) from that same account. On a cold Colorado winter morning, your tenant steps outside, slips and falls, and suffers a traumatic brain injury that renders him incapable of ever working again. He and his family decide to sue you (the property owner) under a premises liability theory. Your landlord insurance policy has a $1 million limit. However, the judgment comes back for $2 million. Taking any appeals out of the equation, your insurance will pay out $1 million.

Because the judgment is against you personally, the tenant (and their attorneys) will now come looking for your assets to satisfy the remaining $1 million of that judgment. They will likely start by forcing the sale of the rental property. They will take whatever is left of the sales proceeds after the mortgage (if any) on that property is satisfied. In most states, they can also force the sale of your primary residence and collect most of the equity there. They can levy your bank and brokerage accounts, garnish your wages, and generally make your financial life a living hell.

Scenario 2

For Scenario 2, we'll keep the initial facts the same. You buy the same Colorado property and rent it to the same tenant – however, this time, you take title to the property in the name of a Colorado LLC. The LLC is properly formed with the state and has a corporate book with ownership interest certificates and a corporate seal, an organizational resolution of the owners, an operating agreement, etc. The rental income goes into a bank account established under the name and Tax ID (Employer Identification Number) of the LLC, and you pay expenses related to the property (insurance, property taxes, maintenance and repairs, etc.) from the LLC account.

The same injury occurs in the same way. Your tenant sues under the same premises liability theory and wins the same $2 million judgment. Your insurance covers the same $1 million. So, what is different? The judgment isn't against you – it's against your Colorado LLC. This means that only the assets of the LLC are at stake to satisfy the remaining $1 million of the judgment. The "LL" in LLC stands for "limited liability." By forming the LLC correctly (and in the correct state) and operating it correctly (i.e., through the separate LLC bank account), you have limited your liability to the assets owned by the entity. So, the tenant will still start collections by forcing the sale of the rental property, and they will still get whatever is left of the sales proceeds after the mortgage (if any) on that property is satisfied. They can also take whatever cash may be in the LLC bank account. However, all your personal assets (my house, bank/brokerage accounts, wages, etc.) are off the table.

LLC structures can get complex when there are multiple properties and large amounts of equity, but at the root, the LLC is there to protect you from the potential liabilities associated with being a landlord – including those not covered by your insurance. More involved LLC structures can also protect individual rental properties (or groups of properties) from each other and enhance the protection of the equity in the rental properties from the LLC owner(s)' personal liabilities.

While I am not an investment advisor, most advisors favor investment diversification. Diversification is the idea of spreading investments across different asset classes, industries, and geographic regions to reduce the overall risk of an investment portfolio. By holding a variety of investments, the poor performance of any one investment can be offset by the better performance of another, leading to a more consistent overall return[112]. Owning investments in both real estate and the stock market can be a great way of achieving diversification across asset classes.

Another "investment" vehicle that is pushed (primarily by insurance salespeople) is whole life insurance. Whole life insurance covers your entire life as long as you keep paying the premiums. It works like a combination of insurance and savings – part of your premium goes to protect your family if something happens to you, and another part goes into a savings account that can grow over time. This savings component is called the "cash value." You can then borrow against the cash value later in life. Because it is a loan that has to be repaid, what you borrow is not taxed. Most folks don't pay the loans back during their lifetime. Instead, they are repaid out of the benefit that would otherwise go to your beneficiaries when you die (the death benefit).

Whole life can be a tool for wealthy individuals who have maxed out 401k, IRA, HSA, and other tax-advantaged accounts and are looking for additional tax-advantaged investments, but for the most part, it should be avoided. Here are the main drawbacks:

1) **It's expensive.** The premiums are significantly more costly than term life policies (discussed in Chapter 6), and a substantial portion of the premium goes towards administrative costs, agent commissions, and policy expenses, leaving a smaller amount to go toward the cash

---

[112] https://www.investopedia.com/investing/importance-diversification/

value and death benefit. Life insurance companies love whole life because it makes them money – not you!

2) **The cash value grows slowly.** While the cash value will grow over time, the returns are often modest compared to other investment opportunities available in the market (such as the stock market and real estate options we have already discussed). Additionally, you'll have to contend with various fees and interest rates that can eat into the overall growth potential. Because of this, I suggest maintaining a (much) cheaper term policy and investing the difference.

3) **It isn't flexible.** Once you commit to a policy, making changes can be complex and involve surrender charges or reductions in benefits. This lack of adaptability will hinder your ability to adjust your coverage as your financial circumstances evolve.

Staying "Intentional" as You Age

Long-Term Care Considerations

An important part of being intentional about building wealth is planning for expenses that can decimate what you have built. One significant example is long-term care in a nursing home, assisted living facility, or in your own home. The statistics say that about 70% of us will require long-term care, and the average amount of time we will need it is three years[113]. The average monthly cost for a nursing home is almost $9,000[114]. There are three potential solutions to this problem:

1) **Government Programs.** Medicare does not cover long-term nursing home or skilled nursing facility care. Medicaid

---

[113] https://acl.gov/ltc/basic-needs/how-much-care-will-you-need
[114] https://www.genworth.com/aging-and-you/finances/cost-of-care/cost-of-care-trends-and-insights.html

will, but only if you qualify. To qualify, your income and assets must be below certain thresholds. Most people will need to "spend down" their assets to qualify for assistance. There are also planning opportunities through contributing assets to certain types of Medicaid Asset Protection Trusts, so they are no longer considered yours for Medicaid qualification purposes.

2) **Self-insurance**. <u>This is the goal</u>. Being self-insured means you have created a nest egg large enough that it (and the income it generates) can easily cover any long-term care costs. You don't have to rely on the government to care for you. You don't have to "spend down" assets. You don't need to pay attorneys to play games with your assets to qualify for Medicaid. You've got it covered.

3) **Long-term care insurance.** We are shooting for self-insurance. However, depending on your particular situation, you may never get there. It's also possible that you would have gotten there, but your health wouldn't cooperate, and you need long-term care before you achieve self-insurance. Are you stuck relying on the government? Nope. This is where long-term care insurance comes in. This insurance covers nursing home and other types of care if they ever become necessary. Waiting to buy it until you need care doesn't work. A good rule of thumb is to purchase long-term care insurance when you turn 60 (unless you feel comfortable that you are already self-insured). When you reach the goal of self-insurance, drop the policy.

Reverse Mortgages

<u>The reverse mortgage is one (frankly harmful) financial product sold to older Americans</u>. They are a way for older folks (age 62 and above) to borrow money based on the equity in their home. Because the reverse mortgage proceeds must be repaid, they are

not taxed and do not affect your Social Security or Medicare benefits. Sounds great – sign me up, right?! Not so fast.

First, reverse mortgages are notoriously expensive when it comes to fees and other costs. Next, with a reverse mortgage, the lender will send you funds in one lump sum payment, a series of monthly payments, or some combination of the two. But regardless of how the money gets to you, the lender adds interest each month to your principal balance. That means the balance increases over time, increasing the amount that must eventually be repaid. Consequently, as time passes, you will have less and less equity in your home. Finally, please be aware that the reverse mortgage loan must be repaid when you die or move out of the home. This may limit your ability to relocate to be closer to family, downsize, or move into a nursing home. At the very least, it will reduce (and possibly eliminate) what your heirs will receive from the sale of the house when you pass away.

For these reasons, I never suggest entering into a reverse mortgage arrangement.

Estate Planning

I want to close things by talking about Estate Planning. I think this makes sense because the primary goal of Estate Planning is to ensure that your assets go where you want them to when you die. Therefore, your Estate Plan is your final intentional financial act on this earth. This is why I always tell clients: "<u>I don't care when you do their Estate Plan – as long as you do it before you die. However, because none of us know precisely when that might be, I suggest you complete your Estate Plan right now!</u>"

In a nutshell, Estate Planning is the art of continuing to prosper when you're alive and passing your property to your loved ones with a minimum of fuss and expense after you die. Planning your estate will typically involve creating a will, a living trust, health care directives, and durable powers of attorney for health care and finances.

There are many myths about Estate Planning – so let's take a minute to dispel some of them.

Myth #1 - I'm too young to worry about Estate Planning. This is true – until it isn't. Accidents, suicides, and illnesses take people in the prime of life every day. When you don't take the time to plan, those left behind are left with a mess.

Myth #2 – I don't need an estate plan because my family will "do the right thing." In my career, <u>I have seen a lot of strange things happen at the intersection of family and money</u>. When a payday is on the horizon, things like loyalty and honesty often go out the window. Otherwise trustworthy people can become decidedly less so when they have dollar signs in their eyes. <u>But let's go ahead and assume that everyone's actions and intentions are 100% pure – your family still won't know what the "right thing" is if you haven't told them</u>. And heaven forbid that you said one thing once and another thing some other time. Your written Estate Planning documents are how your loved ones know what "the right thing" is.

Myth #3 – I don't need an Estate Plan because my spouse will inherit everything anyway, and that's what I want. Maybe. Maybe not. Is this your first marriage? Do you have children from another relationship? If so, your spouse won't necessarily get everything. What happens if your spouse gets remarried after you die? What if your spouse decides to change up what you think you've agreed upon after you die? These are issues a well-drafted Estate Plan will deal with.

Myth #4 – Only the mega-wealthy need a detailed estate plan. Do you own your home or a small business? If so, an Estate Plan with a living trust can save your heirs thousands of dollars in attorney's fees and court costs, and months of time in dealing with those assets when you're gone.

Myth #5 – I don't need to worry about an Estate Plan – I don't have anyone to leave my assets to. Guess what – the law will find someone. It could be a half-sibling you never met or a cousin who drove you crazy as a kid. If there really is no one, your assets will "escheat" to the coffers of the state where you reside when you pass away. I can't think of anyone who finds that an appealing option. Think about causes you are passionate about – maybe a church or a charity. You can make those causes the beneficiaries of your estate and feel good about how your assets will be used when you're gone.

There are three primary options for what to do when it comes to Estate Planning. Let's go through them:

1) **The first one is easily the most popular – DO NOTHING!!!** About two-thirds of Americans choose this option[115]. Why? Mainly because it's easy (what could be easier than doing nothing!), and most people just don't want to think about it. This is true even of very famous and wealthy people. One example is the singer, Prince. He died in 2016 with no trust, no will, no Estate Plan whatsoever. His estate was valued at just over $156 million!

2) **Do a will only.** A will is a document in which you specify who will receive your property at your death and name an executor to effectuate those wishes. You should also use your will to name a guardian for your young children. To be valid, a will must be signed by the person who made it (called the testator), dated, and witnessed by two people.

---

[115] https://www.cnbc.com/2022/04/11/67percent-of-americans-have-no-estate-plan-heres-how-to-get-started-on-one.html

3) **Complete a Comprehensive Estate Plan.** A Comprehensive Estate Plan includes the following documents:

- **A Financial Power of Attorney** – which will name people to make financial decisions on your behalf if you ever become incapacitated.
- **A Healthcare Power of Attorney** – which will name people to make medical decisions on your behalf if you ever become incapacitated.
- **A Living Will (also known as an Advance Health Care Directive)** – which (if desired) will direct medical providers to end life-sustaining care for you if specific parameters are met (such as being in a persistent, vegetative state).
- **A Will** – which will still name a guardian for any young children. However, this one will state that all assets will be distributed as your trust directs.
- **A Revocable Living Trust** – which will specify who will receive your assets (and when and how) when you pass away. The trust will also name a successor trustee who will have the authority to effectuate the instructions in the trust language.

While your Estate Planning decisions will answer several important questions, the one people seem to be most concerned with is: <u>How will my assets be distributed upon my passing, and who will facilitate the distribution of those assets?</u> The answer depends on which of the three Estate Planning options you chose. So, what happens if:

1) **You did nothing.** Your assets will be distributed <u>according to the "intestacy laws" of the state where you reside at the time of your death</u>. Essentially, "the state decides." Intestacy is the legal term for dying without a will or other

"testamentary" document stating what you want to have done with your assets. Depending on your situation, this statute will divide your assets between a surviving spouse and any surviving descendants. If you don't have either, we start going out to parents, siblings, aunts, uncles, cousins, etc. This is why Prince's estate ended up split among his one full sibling and five half-siblings (as determined by Minnesota statute). The state statute will also determine who is appointed as the "executor" of the estate (also known as a "personal representative"). The executor will administer the estate's assets as the statute directs.

2) **You did a will only.** Your assets will be distributed <u>as you direct in the language of the will</u>. You have very few opportunities in life to make the law. Deciding who will get your stuff when you die is one of them. When you make a valid will, you take advantage of that chance. You will name an executor for your estate who will administer the estate's assets as the will directs. So, what's the problem with only doing a will? One word – probate. Probate is a legal process overseen by a probate court judge in which the judge determines whether the will was entered into and executed correctly and given legal effect. If so, the judge will issue an order stating that ruling and appoint the executor. If not, the estate will be deemed "intestate," – and things will proceed as if the deceased had no will. The problem is the time, expense, and headache of going through the probate process to effectuate your wishes. Probate matters usually take 3-6 months to wind through the legal process (even in simple, uncontested cases). They also cost several thousand dollars in court costs and legal fees. Until the process works itself out, no one can do anything with the estate's assets. Perhaps the real estate market is hot, and putting Mom's old house on the market right now will spark a bidding war that will substantially increase the home's sales price. Too bad. No one can do anything with the house until the probate

"clears."

3) **You completed a comprehensive estate plan.** Your assets will be distributed <u>as you direct in the language of your trust</u>. Just like with a will, you have taken advantage of the rare opportunity to make the law (about who gets your stuff). The major difference is that you will have saved your heirs the time, expense, and headache of going through the probate process. You can list Mom's house almost immediately. Let the bidding war commence! Assets can be sold, distributed, and administered without waiting for probate to clear – because there is no probate! You will have saved your heirs thousands of dollars and months of time!

Once your Estate Plan is in place, make sure to check in on it every 2-3 years. A correctly structured plan will allow you to make changes as they become necessary. When you review your documents, ask yourself the following questions:

- Do you still want the same beneficiaries?
- Does it still make sense to distribute assets that way?
- Do you still want the same people in charge of effectuating your wishes after you die (or making financial and medical decisions for you if you ever become incapacitated)?

<u>Final Thoughts</u>

Step 7 is not about money or "getting rich." It's about arriving at a place where you feel freedom and peace instead of feeling fear and anxiety about your finances. You got here by making intentional decisions about your finances. <u>Don't stop now!</u> As you continue to be intentional in spending, giving away, and investing your money, you will find you are able to slow down and enjoy life. Your relationships will be less transactional and more meaningful. And, most importantly, you can use your wealth to bless the lives of your family and those closest to you – as well as some people you barely know!

That freedom, that peace, is why you chose to sacrifice during Steps 1-3. It's why you continued to save and invest in Steps 4-6. Now that you're here in Step 7 (or once you get here), take time to reflect on the journey and feel some genuine pride for what you have accomplished. You've shown an ability to delay what might feel good now for a brighter financial future. That ability is rare indeed. <u>However, with great privilege comes great responsibility</u>. Your responsibility is to pass on the principles of financial success to others – starting with your children (whether they're grown or not). Instill in them the desire to live intentionally when it comes to their finances. Give them the tools and roadmap to travel the same path you have (and maybe to do it even more efficiently). Don't be a nag, but please don't shy away from sharing what you know. Sharing what you know, and maybe even sharing this book, may literally change someone's life. You have that power!

Stop Choosing

- **To believe that spending money is evil.** You went through all of the sacrifices of the previous steps so you would have extra cash now – don't feel guilty about spending it! Be intentional and continue making a budget each month, but I absolutely want you to spend more money than you did in Steps 1-3!

- **Get rich-quick schemes and investments that are "too good to be true."** There are plenty of investment scams out there. Please watch out for the following:

    - **High-Pressure Sales Tactics.** If you have to act now to invest, don't invest at all.
    - **Promises of Crazy Profits.** If it seems too good to be true, it almost certainly is.
    - **Claims that the Investment Is Risk-Free.** "Guaranteed"

returns and assurances that you "can't go wrong" are excellent signs that you are being conned.
- o **Evasive Answers and Lack of Communication.** A failure to provide details and a disclosure document or to respond directly to your questions should diminish your enthusiasm for any investment.
- o **Investments You Don't Understand.** Beware of anyone who tells you that the specifics are "too technical" to describe in layman's terms or that the information is "classified" or "confidential." The promoter is likely just blowing smoke, and you probably don't want to be involved anyway if it's really that complicated.

- **Extremes in the use of debt to fund real estate investments.** "Maximizing leverage" to make real estate investments will maximize the pain when prices fall, renters default, pandemics hit, HVAC systems fail, and roofs fall apart. However, waiting until you can pay for real estate investments 100% in cash may cause you to miss out on some potentially fantastic opportunities. My rule of thumb is to be twice as careful as the banks require and put at least 40% down on any real estate investment.

Start Choosing

- **Generosity.** Your intentional financial decisions have landed you in a spot where you can look outward to find those in your community who need a hand. Please take advantage of those opportunities as they present themselves and reap the mental and physical health benefits.

- **To invest.** We build true wealth in this country by investing. Do your homework about stock market, real estate, and other investment options – and get going!

- **To make the law about who gets your stuff when you pass away.** You don't get many chances to make the law, but this is one of them. Take the time to decide who gets your assets and how. Use a trust to help your heirs avoid the time, expense, and headache of the probate process.

ABOUT THE AUTHOR

Jarom is a Senior Attorney at KKOS Lawyers in Cedar City, Utah, where he has worked since 2011. He focuses his practice on helping clients save taxes, protect their assets, raise business capital, navigate self-directing their retirement, and ensure their loved ones are taken care of after they pass away. His clients are entrepreneurs, small business owners, and real estate investors from all across the country and all walks of life. He and his wife paid off $221,000 of non-mortgage debt in 31 months by living the principles explained in *Stop Choosing to Be Broke: A User's Guide to Money*. Jarom is also the author of an adorable children's book available on Amazon called *Why Do Witches Wear Black?* He lives in beautiful Southern Utah with his wife and three children.

www.ingramcontent.com/pod-product-compliance
Lightning Source LLC
Chambersburg PA
CBHW050908160426
43194CB00011B/2322